LIVING
KINDNESS

LIVING KINDNESS

THE BUDDHA'S TEN GUIDING
PRINCIPLES FOR A BLESSED LIFE

DONALD ALTMAN

INNER
OCEAN

Inner Ocean Publishing, Inc.
P.O. Box 1239
Makawao, Maui, HI 96768-1239

Cover design: Bill Greaves
Cover photo: The Image Bank
Interior page design: Bill Greaves
Interior page typography: Madonna Gauding
Copy editor: Barbara Doern Drew

Publisher Cataloging-in-Publication Data

Altman, Donald.
    Living kindness : the Buddha's ten guiding principles for a blessed life / Donald Altman ; foreword by Lama Surya Das. — 1st ed.—Makawao, HI : Inner Ocean, 2003.

    p. ; cm.

    Includes bibliographical references.
    ISBN 1-930722-23-0
    1. Bodhisattva stages (Mahayana Buddhism). 2. Religious life—Mahayana Buddhism. 3. Spiritual life—Buddhism. 4. Mahayana Buddhism. I. Das, Surya. II. Title.

BQ4330 .A48 2003
294.3444–dc21   0309 CIP

Printed in Canada by Transcontinental
Distributed by Publishers Group West

9 8 7 6 5 4 3 2 1

May this work be a blessing
For all those who strive for awakening,
And for all spiritual sages and enlightened ones
Who bring light into the darkness

Contents

Acknowledgments

This book is a blessing that has been touched and influenced by many. My deep appreciation and gratitude go to all who have shared their feedback and ideas.

In particular, my spiritual friend and brother Ashin Thitzana, whose knowledge, compassion, and insight were invaluable; Lama Surya Das, for so generously giving of his time, wisdom, and support; U Thondara and the monks and community of the Burma Buddhist Monastery; the venerable U Silananda, for his compassionate teaching on behalf of all seekers; Lama John Makransky, for sharing resources; Randy Fitzgerald, a friend and writing confidante; my agents, Arielle Ford and Brian Hilliard, for their friendship, guidance, and creativity; Greg Crosby, for sharing his enlightened teachings; Cynthia Altman, Brad Anderson, Paul O'Brien, Connie Hill, and Rita Shapiro, for their heartfelt stories of living kindness; coeditorial director John Nelson, for his passionate support of my vision for *Living Kindness*; copy editor Barbara Doern Drew, for her insights, suggestions, and enthusiasm; publisher John Elder and the entire staff at Inner Ocean Publishing, for all their efforts; and to all those too numerous to mention, for their kind words and thoughts.

Thanks also to my father, Norman. Especially, I am grateful for the extraordinary living kindness of my mother, Barbara, and the love of my life, Sanda.

Foreword
The Heart of Enlightenment: Transforming Ourselves, Transforming the World

It was in 1999, shortly after reading and enjoying his book *Art of the Inner Meal,* that I met Donald Altman for the first time—appropriately, over a meal. In the years that have followed we have had the opportunity to visit and share ideas many times. Donald has always shown himself to be a knowledgeable and genuine seeker in his spiritual pursuits. He cares deeply about the impact and benefit that his work can provide for others.

A year after our initial meeting, while in Portland for my *Awakening to the Sacred* book tour, I had another meal with Donald and his wife, Sanda. It was on that occasion that he told me about his new book and that it would be based on the "perfections" (*paramitas* in Sanskrit), or transcendental virtues, that comprise a manual for awakening and engaging in a truly good life. My first impression was that here is someone who is diligent in practicing these virtues, who understands and embraces them, and who can make them accessible to others. In short, he is a Bodhisattva:

what my late father would have called a real mensch—a genuine human being.

Living Kindness confirms the ancient virtues as indispensable tools for shaping a compassionate twenty-first century. It is with a distinct sense of clarity, humor, and wisdom that these pages bring to life the very principles used by Gautama Siddhartha, the historical Buddha (563–483 B.C. in India), to attain his enlightenment. Perhaps the most unique aspect of this book is its broadened perspective on the perfections as universal virtues that can awaken and benefit all. For that reason, the words and ideas of the Buddha are complemented by the wisdom of Gandhi, Jesus, Inayat Khan, Saint Francis, and many well-known Buddhist teachers. As such, this interfaith book serves as a valuable and inspiring source for anyone who wants to directly experience the transcendent virtues in daily life.

As Donald describes the perfections, they are at once simple and complex. They tell us how to integrate the outer, inner, and innate levels of enlightened living and carry all circumstances into our path—how to integrate and assimilate everything we experience into spiritual learning, growth, and development. Traditionally, these principles are taught as a form of training, going through virtues from the more easy to the more difficult and from the gross to the subtle; but more profoundly, and seen from the bigger perspective, they are the enlightened way of living itself. They are not just steps leading up to awakening, they *are* it.

In a more general sense, these principles of enlightened living are a process of developing ourselves that we can apply in life, thus becoming wiser and more compassionate, more sane rather than more conflicted or disturbed, more balanced and whole, and more helpful rather than harmful. On the other hand, the paramitas embody and enact the way of transcendental wisdom itself. Each of them *is* wise, *is* totally perfect, and embodies all the other enlightened qualities in itself. This is what distinguishes them from ordinary virtues or mere goodness. Most fundamentally, as this book expresses, these principles "give us the means for 'living kindness.'"

In Buddhism, the Ten Paramitas are the code of the altruistic spiritual seeker, the Bodhisattva—literally an "enlightening being," or an awakening spiritual practitioner. It was through practicing these ten transcendental virtues over the course of numerous lifetimes that the Buddha himself said that he achieved perfect complete enlightenment and Nirvana. Over the millennia, countless beings have progressed in enlightenment through cultivating and applying these principles of enlightened living in their lives and to the benefit of their worlds.

Historically, the original scriptures of Buddhism, the Sutras (spoken by Buddha), laid out the Ten Paramitas (*paramis* in Pali), which correspond respectively to each of the ten *bhumis* (stages, grounds) of the Bodhisattva path. (Buddhahood, full enlightenment, is the eleventh bhumi.) The Mahayana teaching as taught by my own Tibetan masters usually teaches the Six Paramitas, to simplify the practice as six principles for Bodhisattvas to practice as part of their Bodhisattva Vow, a code by which to live that is included and explained in *Living Kindness.*

As described in this book, the paramitas are guidelines, touchstones, inspirations rather than rules or precepts (as in "Thou shalt not"). Practicing these spiritual perfections, sublime values, or selfless noble powers helps us develop in wisdom and compassion, truth and love, as well as promising, according to traditional sources, better rebirths with favorable conditions.

Living Kindness offers many examples of the benefits and blessings to be gained by practicing to perfection these principles. My lamas have said that generosity, for example, results in the enjoyment of ample material resources, now and later. Effort endows us with the ability to complete what we undertake. Patience leads to supportive companions and better appearance. Ethical self-discipline provides a free and well-endowed rebirth as well as greater attractiveness and more relaxation in this life. Meditation and concentration make the mind invulnerable to distraction. Wisdom helps us discriminate between what should be undertaken and what should be abandoned. Truthfulness keeps us in harmony with others, furthers character and integrity, and brings rebirth in higher, divine realms of existence. Steadfastness stabilizes our hearts and minds, improves all our relationships, and reliably directs us toward spiritual opportunities in the future. Equanimity likewise provides balance and stability, helps us stay on course in the long run, and furthers healthy living. Loving-kindness is the greatest protection from evil and the ultimate gift to others, and it directs us to nirvanic peace, bliss, and divine love.

Most importantly, the paramitas are multidimensional in their ability to change our lives. That point is illustrated throughout *Living Kindness*. In meditation, for example, we may seem to be sitting by ourselves, but we do not sit just for ourselves. As we wake up to reality, we become a force for universal awakening through the Ten Perfections as wisdom's enactment in the form of compassion in action. Such is the power of embracing the paramitas.

We live in dangerous times. Martin Luther King said that we have two choices: to peacefully coexist or to destroy ourselves. The true battlefield is the heart of man, as Dostoevsky stated. If we want peace in the world—and I firmly believe that we all do—we need to face this fact and learn how to soften up and disarm our own hearts, as well as work toward nuclear disarmament and peace in our time. The opening words of the UNESCO Charter are: "Since wars begin in the human mind, it is in that mind that peace must be defended and constructed."

How can we become a real friend to all the world's people? How can we be a guardian and an advocate for the disenfranchised, oppressed, and downtrodden, including those who oppose us? We must learn to deal with our own anger, hatred, prejudices, delusions, greed, and fear. Buddha said, "See yourself in others, and others in yourself; then whom can you harm, whom can you exploit?" Awakening to living kindness through the paramitas offers more than a step in the right direction; it is a step toward a blessing filled life for all.

In closing, I offer a Bodhisattva prayer from the original Tibetan:

From now until enlightenment is reached, now and
    through all my lifetimes
I go for refuge in the Buddha, the Dharma and the
    Sangha;
May I wholeheartedly practice the Six Perfections
For the boundless benefit of one and all.

Lama Surya Das
Dzogchen Center
Cambridge, Massachusetts

Introduction: *Touchstones for the Spirit*

The perfume of sandalwood,
Rosebay or jasmine
Cannot travel against the wind.
But the fragrance of virtue
Travels even against the wind,
As far as the ends of the world.

Like garlands woven from a heap of flowers,
Fashion from your life as many good deeds.

—Buddha, *Dhammapada*

During my first morning in the monastery I am stirred awake by an eerie sound. Several voices, speaking as one, echo in the predawn darkness. Am I dreaming? Slowly, my mind clears. The monks in the nearby meditation room chant in long, drawn-out monochromatic tones. Their voices—some low and

deep and raspy, others smooth and melodic—unite in a se-
rene, yet haunting, harmony.

Mesmerized, I lie in bed, soothed for more than thirty
minutes by the very sound and energy of Pali words that I do
not understand, but that somehow speak to me:

> Practice that consumes evil states, a noble life, seeing the
> Noble Truths and realization of Nibbana. This is the high-
> est blessing.

> The mind of a person who is confronted with worldly
> conditions does not flutter, is sorrowless, stainless and
> secure. This is the highest blessing.

> Having fulfilled such things as these, beings are invin-
> cible everywhere and gain happiness everywhere. That
> is the highest blessing for them.[1]

These three verses from the *Mangala Sutta* are but a small
part of the total 164 verses that together form the *paritta pali*,
or protective verses. This collection brings together eleven
different Buddhist *suttas*, or discourses. At one level, these are
devotional chants intended to protect both those who chant
and those who listen. At a deeper level, the lessons of these
ancient verses focus on what is required to awaken the sacred
and live a blessing-filled life. They show us how to untangle
ourselves from suffering by following the example of the Buddha. Most fundamentally, they make a direct point: The way
to be protected from evil, danger, confusion, and complexity
is through diligent, courageous awakening to the right principles. Once we do this, all the rest falls naturally into place.
But what are the right guiding principles?

Any useful set of principles must be practical and functional. Such principles must guide us to a more consciously aware and sensitive life. They must give us the tools for spreading compassion and blessings all around us. They need to help us live a life that truly matters, both for ourselves and others. In other words, they must give us the means for "living kindness."

Living kindness is not some hypothetical idea. It is the artful, daily expression of kindness, compassion, and deep respect for all beings regardless of differences in faith, belief, culture, gender, social status, and ethnicity. This is kindness with the power of mindful action behind it. Rather than being reduced to a "random acts of kindness" bumper sticker, this kindness is uniquely boundless, purposeful, and empowering. It is also more open and forgiving than the self- sacrificing kindness that I learned about in Sunday school. Living kindness is a vehicle by which our love, generosity, and other vital values make contact with the real world. This is kindness where it counts. While the term and concept of living kindness are my own, it is best understood and experienced through a set of timeless principles that the Buddha himself followed.

How is it that ancient principles can be relevant for us in this new millennium? How can we know that living kindness as practiced by the Buddha, Jesus, and other virtuous beings is not some historical artifact? It is true that we enjoy many more comforts in daily living than even a hundred years ago. Still, despite all our wonderful advancements in medicine, computers, aviation, and other areas, the twentieth century was also the most violent period in human history. All the technology in the world cannot tell us how to fill our lives with blessings. It cannot heal our emotional and spiritual wounds. It cannot answer our most pressing ethical questions, especially those that affect our inner and external peace and happiness.

At the same time, we can take heart: the hard lessons of the past have induced wise and compassionate beings throughout history to seek practical solutions. Living kindness is a solution that should not be underestimated. For as Robert Louis Stevenson once wrote, "It is the history of our kindnesses that alone makes this world tolerable. If it were not for that, for the effect of kind words, kind looks, kind letters . . . I should be inclined to think our life a practical jest in the worst possible spirit."[2]

Living Kindness focuses on wise, timeless, and enduring spiritual principles, or values, that were promoted and followed by the historical Gautama Buddha. The *Buddha Vamsa Pali Texts*, or lineage of the Buddhas, tell the story of how the Buddha-to-be found the ten conditions necessary for becoming a Buddha. These principles are astonishingly fresh and easily adapted to modern life. Some Buddhist teachings use these as their ideal, a means by which one becomes a Bodhisattva, or an "awakening being" seeking enlightenment. But do not assume that this makes them exclusively "Buddhist" principles or standards. Or that you have to be a Bodhisattva to experience them.

Who can benefit from these principles? Anyone can. Whatever your faith, creed, or background, living kindness represents an inclusive, tolerant, and interfaith path that is not steeped in dogma or ideology. These ten principles—generosity, effort, patience, ethics, simplicity and meditation, wisdom, truthfulness, steadfastness, equanimity, and loving-kindness—offer a universal path to spiritual growth and compassionate living kindness. They can also help us cope with the many challenges facing us today, both personally and as a community.

TAKING LIVING KINDNESS HOME

While these values are direct and straightforward, they are infinitely complex, too. That is why living kindness is about *experiencing* and *touching* the ten values. Simply theorizing about them misses the point. This reminds me of one evening when I drove to a large church to hear an internationally known spiritual figure and writer. The auditorium was sold out. Opening prayers and stirring live music got us all in a receptive mood.

The lecturer was as polished and engaging as I had expected. He spoke almost nonstop for more than two hours, explaining how modern science supports the concept that we are all spiritually connected and capable of manifesting miracles. It was a marvelous and valuable presentation worthy of the standing ovation it received! Yet when it came time to leave, the parking lot was in a state of mayhem. In the haste to manifest a rapid exit, a rush-hour mind-set took hold, and many drivers refused to let others merge. It seemed to me that while the audience had heard the message, too few were taking it home.

The power of living kindness stems from how it encourages us to embrace and grasp the fullness of all our thoughts, acts, and deeds. That includes even the most seemingly insignificant ones, such as our driving habits. Fundamentally, this translates into taking living kindness home with us. There is just no way to separate the practice of living kindness from daily living; it is all part of the same fabric. In that sense, this work is never really finished. Personally, I will always consider myself a student of this ongoing master's class on spiritual knowledge and growth. Just when I think I have graduated, I receive another lesson that furthers my understanding of living kindness.

This also means that we do not need to make wholesale changes to our lives, give up all our possessions, or move into the forest to meditate. We can simply approach each moment with greater attentiveness, awareness, and appreciation. Suppose, for example, that I give money to a particular charity. As a result I might think, Well, since I make a donation each year, I have done my share of giving. Yet if we adopt this line of thinking, how can we possibly recognize other areas where our giving is stilted or limited? Or suppose my employer asks me to do something that is dishonest or unjust? Again, I might be tempted to rationalize, It's not really my fault because I'm just following company policy. So instead of being fully awake, our spirits are numbed into submissiveness, into slumber. We risk losing our spontaneity, joy, and love of life.

We are not put on this planet to be mindless. Our divine, conscious gifts can be utilized by seeing, hearing, thinking, and feeling with all our potential. This means that we need to use our living kindness intelligence in new and creative ways, instead of falling into the same old patterns of approaching work, family, and life. How do we break free of rigid, frozen thought? What do we gain when we follow the latest trend or play the role that society gives us of boss, parent, or lover, all without recognizing even the most subtle of consequences?

To help us shake off the slumber and reconnect with our divine intelligence is the purpose of living kindness. What is more, a virtue-filled life is an exquisite starting point for anyone who undertakes a spiritual journey.

TEN TOUCHSTONES FOR THE SPIRIT

Although the Buddha's ancient principles are the focal point of this book, the stories and exercises draw upon the world's wisdom traditions, including Hinduism, Buddhism, Judaism, Christianity, Islam, Native American sacred practices, and others. To that end, living kindness confirms what mystics and seekers have long known: that spiritual truths and virtues are not the sole possession of any one tradition, but a treasure to be shared by all.

Living Kindness begins with "Guideposts," a chapter that explores the root meanings of these ancient tools. The unique qualities and properties of the principles are what distinguish them from ordinary virtues or values. By recognizing these qualities, we can more fully experience what the principles have to offer.

The remainder of Living Kindness follows along with the ten timeless principles. "Principle 1: Generosity" focuses on giving, altruism, and charity. In Buddhist texts, this principle is traditionally placed at the top of the list. That is because altruism, letting go of attachments, and diminishing self-centeredness and greed are central to spiritual growth. It is also first on the list because generosity is one of the easier principles to practice. By gently and persistently letting go, we keep from focusing on ourselves—a true obstacle to awakening. We will also explore other views on generosity, from Judaism's degrees of charity to the Native American practice of the "giveaway." This chapter asks us to consider how giving and receiving, whether through service or material means, are both vital parts of the same life-affirming process.

To further anchor and ground our generosity practice in the real world, guided experiences, or exercises, are included throughout this chapter, as well as every chapter. I prefer to use the word experiences rather than practices because the essence of each is to encourage deeper, spontaneous understanding and use of the principles.

"Principle 2: Effort" explores how to effectively use

effort on the path to the ancient principles. Energy is the essence of living beings. Effort, vigor, and enthusiasm—physical, spiritual, and mental—can channel that energy firmly onto the right path and keep us free of distractions. To that end, this chapter shows how to pinpoint and avoid the major obstacles that can derail our effort. It will also explore the importance of vows and how they can be used as tools to strengthen both commitment and discipline.

"Principle 3: Patience" shows how to develop a daily awareness of patience, forbearance, and tolerance. Here, we will examine how harmful expectations and thinking can cause impatience, intolerance, and anger. It will also offer some practical tools for building the inner strength required to forbear from criticizing and complaining about others, as well as learning how to cultivate compassion for ourselves.

"Principle 4: Ethics" illustrates how the right actions and right choices make a difference in each moment, both for ourselves and others. This chapter will show how meaningful precepts can serve as guardians—protecting and preserving our relationships at home, at work, and in the community. We will also learn to recognize and avoid unskillful ways of living that can hinder our spiritual progress and experience of these timeless values. Ethics and virtue are not something to be applied only under certain conditions. Instead, they are essential to maintaining harmony in all our daily relationships and environments.

"Principle 5: Simplicity and Meditation" shows how to cultivate a simpler, stress-free, and joy-filled life. Transformational methods of spiritual reflection and contemplation, especially traditional meditation, will be covered here. With step-by-step guidance, we will learn to heighten our capacity for concentration, awareness, observation, and listening. This principle is vital because it cuts through the illusion of an individual, separate self to reveal the deeper truth of inter-connectedness. This enriching principle can reduce the confusion and complexity in our lives to a point where we can live with greater simplicity, ease, inner peace, and calm.

"Principle 6: Wisdom" is critical because even with all our advanced technology, we still need wisdom to guide us. This chapter focuses on how to develop an inner wisdom that elevates the thinking mind into the knowing mind. Also included is an exploration of the "crazy wisdom" of Tibet's "holy fools"—yogis who use divinely inspired pranks and craziness to break through ignorance and hypocrisy. The experiences included here help to cultivate nonjudgmental awareness, inner strength, and our own crazy wisdom. Truly, the wisdom of the sages (and the ages) is available for each and every one of us to tap into.

"Principle 7: Truthfulness" centers on what it means to live a life with integrity, where truth embodies not only speech, but all our actions. This virtue has been undermined throughout our culture in many ways and through many rationalizations. Yet whenever we undermine the truth, we only diminish our personal authenticity and spiritual growth. This chapter challenges us to distinguish between truth that is self-serving, personal, and conventional, and a powerful and penetrating truth that serves.

"Principle 8: Steadfastness" generates an unshakeable will toward meeting spiritual goals. Without this principle, it might be very difficult, if not impossible, to climb the steep path before us. We should not worry, though, because we are in good company. Buddha and Jesus, for example, faced many temptations and distractions on their journeys. This chapter seeks to answer questions such as, How do we go about strengthening not just our willpower but our "skillpower" on a daily basis? Is it possible to be resolute but not stubborn?

Once we experience what is needed to attain steadfastness, our spiritual, emotional, and material goals will be more easily reached.

"Principle 9: Equanimity" affirms the importance of all living beings, without discrimination. The world in this new millennium is unlike any other time in history. We understand better than ever that the actions we take can have long-reaching ramifications that go beyond our neighborhoods, our counties, our states, and our countries. To experience equanimity is to set aside many of our long-conditioned attitudes. Equanimity means we can decide how we want to react to the world around us. It asks us to expand our view into one that is more tolerant, unselfish, accepting, and global in scope.

"Principle 10: Loving-Kindness" gives an account of the Buddha's powerful and ancient practice of *metta*, or loving-kindness. Loving-kindness differs greatly from romantic, sentimental, and nostalgic love. Experiencing this virtue of encompassing goodwill can help us tap into the unlimited and creative energy of divine love that binds us all together. And, since loving-kindness often requires a sense of forgiveness, this chapter will open new doorways for self-forgiveness and mercy. Included are chants and blessings that will enable us to transmit loving-kindness to all beings. This nourishing principle truly is a joyful way for us to express our living kindness.

Throughout, I have included some simple spiritual truths from the *Dhammapada*, a collection of the Buddha's own teachings, as well as excerpts from other wise spiritual teachers. These verses combine a shining, laserlike commentary with a sublime sense of wisdom and wit that gently beckon us toward the philosophy of the Buddha himself. Imagine him, or your favorite compassionate guide, greeting you at each unfamiliar turn in the road.

BEYOND THE ABSOLUTES
OF RIGHT AND WRONG

The decision to undertake and explore the ten ancient principles is a matter of personal choice. These are not intended as inflexible moral laws of right and wrong written in stone from above, like the Bible's Ten Commandments. This is not to say, however, that spiritual values are relativistic and to be applied only when they suit our needs! We need to have a set of useful ethical guidelines for choosing how to act under particular circumstances. Certainly, the Buddha's ten principles do this by guiding us into a place of awareness, and from such a place we can choose our actions and thoughts based on self-knowledge, discriminating wisdom, and a humble appreciation for the consequences. This alone can change our worldview, even how we relate to a butterfly, a delicate flower, or a single blade of grass.

At the same time, we need to recognize that we can be thrown off the track whenever we chain our minds to absolutes like "right" and "wrong" or "good" and "evil." It is helpful to remember that life constantly blends the good with the bad, and that even good and kind people may have habits such as drinking, smoking, or unhealthy eating. Likewise, what person is only evil, having never done a single action that could be viewed as having value? Living kindness helps awaken us to all parts of our being. In his classic book *Awakening the Buddha Within*, Lama Surya Das writes, "The problem is that most of us are sleeping Buddhas. To reach enlightenment, our only task is to awaken to who and what we really *are*—and in so doing to become fully awake and conscious in the most profound sense of the word. 'When I am enlightened, all are enlightened,' Buddha said. Help yourself and you help the entire world."[3]

That is why interpreting these timeless principles as strict moral codes to be followed at all costs misses the bigger picture. When that happens we can get stuck in conflict, using our minds to struggle between opposites and dualities, spending our precious energy constantly weighing one thing against another. We also put ourselves in jeopardy of becoming rigid and self-righteous regarding our own points of view. As a result of playing the conflict game, we may unfairly label others (or ourselves) in narrowly defined ways. I am not saying we do not need to use our faculties of discrimination or analytic thought. It is when we are unhappy because of it, or when it keeps us from accepting the truth or learning more about ourselves, that we need to find other, more positive alternatives.

For example, is there someone in your life who provokes you to take a stand on issues? Someone who is a genius button pusher? If you find yourself forced to defend a point of view in order to be right, then you are in another version of the conflict game. And, really, who wins? The Buddha expresses this in his own inimitable way:

> The winner sows hatred
> Because the loser suffers.
> Let go of winning and losing
> And find joy.[4]

Working with these guiding principles can help you discover how a meaningful conversation and relationship can thrive when *neither party has to be right*. Imagine the freedom that comes from acknowledging another's point of view from a place of equanimity, compassion, and acceptance that "this is what he or she thinks and the way things are." None of us needs to be entrapped in a spider's web of right, wrong, winner, and loser.

So, while the Buddha's principles serve a similar purpose as commandments—to strengthen our character and guide us toward nonharmful and ethically beneficial actions—they also represent a path to enlightenment, awakening, purification, and empowerment. They give us fresh perspective from which to embrace daily living and kindness.

AN OPEN PATH

Michelangelo used chisels to release those timeless figures he knew were hidden and trapped in marble. We, too, can use the Buddha's ten guiding principles as chisels to chip away at confusion and reveal our awakened being within. The word *Buddha*, after all, stands for "one who is awakened." And while the name traditionally symbolizes a kind of honorary title applied to those few who have attained a specific level of Nirvana, or enlightenment, it is really much more inclusive than that. To swim into the stream of living kindness is to recognize that the underlying nature of our being is no different from that of the major league Buddhas—such as the historical Gautama Buddha and Padmasambhava, also known as the "Buddha of Compassion."

Sure, we might like to believe that we can attain heaven, Nirvana, or any other destination by attaching ourselves to a particular set of beliefs. However, acquiring a deep realization of spiritual consciousness and being is not about beliefs or about going anywhere else. When we use these principles to stimulate our spiritual being, we awaken the potential for clarity and sensitivity that all beings possess *right here and now.* As Tibetan-trained lama and Buddhist teacher Ken McLeod once pointedly remarked, "Enlightenment is the end of confusion."[5]

From this perspective, the word *Buddha* represents more than a kind of superhuman being who achieved dizzying heights of divine knowledge and consciousness. The Buddha is also like an ideal form, or seed, that exists within each of us. It requires only the right nourishment, effort, care, and living kindness. This simple truth places all of us on an equal footing as seekers. We are all mystics, all capable of self-realization. Even Buddha himself encouraged each person around him to "be a lamp unto your self." Awakening is not something that can be owned by any group, religious or otherwise. It is available and attainable. However, each individual must take responsibility for journeying the path of awakening that living kindness offers. No one else can take those steps for us.

Of course, people still argue over who is a legitimate Buddhist, Jew, Christian, and so forth. They are attached to their spiritual labels. At the time I took my initiatory vows, I was not hoping to become a Theravada, Mahayana, or any other kind of Buddhist—distinctions that did not even exist during Buddha's lifetime. I was not looking for attachment to a group or set of beliefs, but for freedom and liberation. When I entered the monastery as a monk twice during intensive retreat periods—a practice common to the southeast Theravada Buddhist tradition of Burma and Thailand—what I sought was an honest and caring approach to living that satisfied my deep inner need for wholeness.

What initially drew me to the monastery were the monks who lived there. They possessed a genuine sense of inner joy, wisdom, peace, and compassion. Though I had always been drawn to spiritual teachings, these special qualities were not consistently part of my life at that time. I was in my forties, and a sudden career transition signaled me that the time was right to pursue my spiritual growth and experience such qualities for myself—and, ultimately, for the benefit of others through my writing, teaching, and livelihood.

It was how the monks embodied living kindness that moved me most. They have always made themselves available as spiritual friends. Once, for example, they supported my spiritual growth by letting me live on the monastery grounds for three months while writing my first spiritual book. Their generosity, openness, and compassion made an enduring impression. Perhaps that is why I constantly carry the monastery in my heart.

The actions of living kindness, too, can change us in innumerable and lasting ways. The Buddha taught that if we want to know where we are going to be in the future, we can look at where our lives are *at this very moment*. No matter how we add up all the hundreds of thousands of choices and decisions we make in a lifetime, the only ones we can really do anything about are those before us this instant. To choose living kindness means we are free to let go of the ways we may have missed the point in the past. It also releases us from worrying about the likelihood of repeated mishaps in the future. That is why each of us can carry the guiding principles of living kindness in our hearts, wherever we might happen to be. How liberating!

The right principles, values, and virtues enable us to become the masters of our own fate by planting the seeds —karmic or otherwise—for a more fruitful future. True, we may not always know that our actions are the right ones. Sometimes, what appears to be negative or harmful has a silver lining, or vice versa. Still, the guiding principles enable us to look at both light and shadow. They give us a broad palette of colors from which to artistically experience and paint our world.

The decision to embrace living kindness is one of our greatest blessings and empowerments. That is why this book

is dedicated to the growing number of us who want an inclusive, tolerant, and open approach to our spiritual quest. We
do not even need to consider it a spiritual path if we do not
want to. We can just think of it as a gentle path to seeing reality, finding meaning, making life matter, and increasing the
blessings in our lives. As Krishnamurti wisely advised,

> It is discovery to suddenly see yourself as you actually
> are: greedy, quarrelsome, angry, envious, stupid. To see
> the fact without trying to alter it, just to see exactly what
> you are is an astonishing revelation. . . .
>   Through self-knowledge you begin to find out what
> is God, what is truth, what is that state which is timeless.
> . . . Self-knowledge is the beginning of wisdom. In self-
> knowledge is the whole universe; it embraces all the
> struggles of humanity.[6]

As we deepen our connection to these principles, it is
my hope that, individually and as a spiritual community, we
can answer some vital questions: How can we deeply grasp
that despite our differing appearances and personal attachments, we are really all interconnected? How can we learn to
look beyond the symbols of a particular church, temple, or
monastery to see the common principles that exist in all? Even
more challenging, how can we live in a way that maintains
respect and compassion for the beliefs of others?

Finally, if we are not fully enlightened or awake, at least
we can have an enlightened attitude while on the path toward
living kindness. Rather than worry or obsess about enlightenment, why not be honest and accept that we will have our
good days and our bad? We will have some enlightened moments of living kindness, as well as some dull ones. This

encourages all of us to stay real and experience the moment as it is—not how we want it to be.

I am both humbled and pleased to invite you along on what promises to be a fascinating, joyful, and compassionate journey. It is my hope that you will experience some "good days" of your own with the principles to guide you. Yet as every traveler knows, what you discover on your journey may not be what you imagined. But is not that what makes each journey special? Knowing this, there is no better time than now to set sail toward the shores of living kindness.

Guideposts

Though we share this humble path, alone
How fragile is the heart
Oh give these clay feet wings to fly
To touch the face of the stars.

—Loreena McKennitt,
lyrics from "Dante's Prayer"

A story from India's early Vedic scriptures tells about a man from a small village who was blindfolded and taken out to the wilderness. From these desolate surroundings he cried out for help. A local sage heard his pleas and removed the blindfold. Yet when the man gazed out, he recognized nothing. The landscape was completely foreign to him. And so he stood, frozen in his tracks with no idea which way to turn.

The wise sage, feeling the man's sadness, inquired about the name of the village. Upon hearing the name, the sage simply pointed and said, "Follow that path." Once on the path, the man constantly asked for directions along the way. Each

village he encountered acted as a guidepost that led him farther and farther down the road. After a long and uncertain
journey, he finally reached his homeland. The man had trusted
in the knowledge of those he met, and each new piece of information gave him more evidence that he was headed in the
right direction.

PROPERTIES OF THE
ANCIENT PRINCIPLES

We all need guideposts of one sort or another. As you
experience the ten ancient principles, you will want to know
whether you are headed in the right direction. The ancient
principles possess distinctive properties, or qualities. My suggestion is to become familiar with these, but not to dwell on
them. Regard them as checkpoints rather than destinations.
After all, as the mystic Lao Tzu wrote more than 2,500 years
ago, "A good traveler has no fixed plans and is not intent on
arriving."

The ancient principles trace back to the ancient Pali word
parami. Pali was the Buddha's language from northern India,
and parami pertains to the creation of deeds or mental states
belonging to holy, noble, or spiritually awakened beings. Today, they are often referred to by the Sanskrit word
paramita—usually translated as perfection, virtue, or the highest ideals of spiritual perfection. The paramitas also contain
the essence of the Latin word *perfectio*, which signifies completion or completeness. (While the ancient principles are often
referred to as "perfections," I tend to refer to them as "principles," "values," and "virtues." My reasoning is that these
terms are more widely understood and accessible.)

The principles meld together all of the above definitions.

That is because the ancient principles are best experienced and understood through five unique properties, which differentiate them from these dictionary-defined terms.

1. Each ancient principle illuminates and possesses all ten principles.

This first property makes each principle entirely whole and inseparable from the others. Imagine a single, flawless diamond containing ten brilliant facets, or virtues. Whenever you express any of them, you are really expressing and practicing them all. Being aware of how all the principles are interconnected can also help you explore for yourself whether or not you are experiencing each principle in its perfection.

2. Each principle purifies and strengthens our spiritual growth.

As this second property points out, our character and inner spirit are purified when we intentionally perform holy deeds and actions on a daily basis. Of course, this idea of reaching for spiritual perfection lives in all the wisdom traditions. Early Christianity, for example, adapted Jewish fasts and by the Middle Ages had fully embraced the idea of attaining human spiritual perfection through renunciation and living an ascetic, pious life. In the tradition of Mahayana Buddhism, many laypersons, nuns, and monks willingly take a vow to follow the six (sometimes ten) virtues. By doing so, practitioners purify themselves while at the same relieving the suffering of others through beneficial acts of love and compassion. (The "Bodhisattva Vow" is covered in "Principle 2: Effort.") Because of this property, the ancient principles give us the strength to lead by the right kind of action. They also help us to confront difficult circumstances that might otherwise pressure us to lie, cheat, steal, rationalize, and cause suffering for ourselves and others.

Have we not all felt peer pressure—as teenagers, at work, and at play? I can remember that when I first stopped drinking alcohol as an adult in my thirties, several people mistakenly assumed that I must have had a drinking problem. Today, people rarely ask me why. And if they do, I often explain my vow not to take any substance that could alter my consciousness. Of course, I always add that this is *my* choice—one that is not necessarily right for everyone.

3. Each principle awakens us to the way things really are.

This third quality asks us not to mistake the Buddhist concept of "perfection" for the word *perfectionist* or to assume that we must *be* perfect in our use of these values. All that is asked of us is to make an ongoing effort and commitment to embody these principles, not to be perfect. A failure along the way is not a condemnation. Rather, we need to take each misstep only as a reminder of the way things are, without embellishment or rationalization. This quality brings us to grips with what author Jack Kornfield describes in *After the Ecstasy, the Laundry* as our "ordinary perfection":

> Ordinary perfection is being true to ourselves, to the way things are. Do we go into the garden wishing that the pansies were taller than the daffodils, or thinking that the roses would be fine if only they didn't have thorns? Do we go into a kindergarten and wish that the children would fit into some model of perfection we hold, or can we see that variety makes the beauty of gardens and

humans, that our spiritual task is not to make perfection
but to awaken to the perfection around us.[1]

Imagine what it would be like to look at yourself through
the eyes of Buddha or Jesus. What would he see? Would he
judge you because your hairstyle was out of fashion? Would
he berate you because you expect too much out of yourself?
Or would he just look at you for who you are, appreciating
and accepting your entire being as is—wrinkled or smooth
complexion, unkempt or styled hair, beneficial or selfish
desires?

We are all "as is" human beings. None of us comes fresh
off the assembly line without a scratch. To know this, even for
a moment, with a pinch of grace, wonderment, and acceptance is to understand that each of us possesses our own
ordinary perfection, or virtue. What, who, and where we are
right now is the ordinary perfection that blesses our lives.

4. Each of the principles transforms and empowers.

This fourth property gives us the means for reaching beyond the shore of our daily lives—including those struggles
and choices that push and pull us in all directions. Should I
please my wife and go to that dinner party with her or finish
that project for my boss? How do I change the eating habits
that cause me so much emotional pain? How do we cross over
to the other shore, and what exactly will we find over there?
In other words, where are the ancient principles taking us?

There may no single, conclusive answer. However, should
we want to consider some interesting possibilities, the oppos-
ing shore can be thought of as an ideal that possesses perfect
wholeness and completeness. In this regard, the ancient principles help to transform and complete our spiritual inner

selves, as well as the external world. They help us navigate toward the right choices—those that empower ourselves and others. They let us transform sorrow, frustration, suffering, incompleteness, and mistrust on this shore into joy, fulfillment, wellness, wholeness, and trust on the other shore. The Buddha tells us more about the benefits of such a transformation:

> Even Gods cherish the vigilant Buddhas,
> Meditative, wise, peaceful,
> And free of passions.[2]

This same idea of completion resonates, for example, in the Bible's Book of Genesis, where God gives man "dominion . . . over all the earth." Does not this really imply that our role is an active one of empowerment and of a consciously aware finisher of divine works? Walter Brueggemann, a Bible scholar and author, believes that a more appropriate translation for the word *dominion* would be "stewardship." Certainly, we craft houses from trees, make wine from grapes, and build dams from stone. However, it is a big responsibility for humankind to act wisely, kindly, and judiciously. And it is one that these principles directly address.

5. Each ancient principle raises and broadens our conscious view.

The fifth property tells us that we do not reach the other shore at all! The Buddha once said that we should aspire to be "one who stands neither on this shore, nor any shore, freed from all chains of worry." In this sense, the values help us to transcend the shores of duality altogether, without needing to cling to one shore or the other.

However, it would be a mistake to think that transcending the shores of duality means we are floating aimlessly up that well-known proverbial creek without a paddle. What it does suggest, though, is that through diligent and constant practice of the ancient principles we can be freed from limiting opinions, judgments, prejudices, and beliefs. And that we can glimpse—without dilution or distraction—another kind of unity beyond the ordinary. Vietnamese monk and teacher Thich Nhat Hanh, in his book *Cultivating the Mind of Love*, tells us:

> When you are hammering a nail into a piece of wood, if you accidentally strike your finger, your right hand will put down the hammer and take care of your left hand. There is no discrimination: "I am the right hand giving you, the left hand, a helping hand." Helping the left hand is helping the right hand. That is practice without relying on form, and the happiness that results is boundless. . . .
> . . . If we do the dishes with anger and discrimination, our happiness will be less than a teaspoonful.[3]

Now, as you prepare to work with the ten ancient principles, bear in mind that you always maintain the freedom to stand upon this shore, that shore, or neither. On this path, the choice is always yours.

Experience: *Feel the Principles of Those You Admire*

This experience should take anywhere from five to twenty minutes. As preparation, find a quiet place to sit, either on a chair or a meditation cushion. Once you are in place, take a deep breath in. Breathe out, letting out a loud *AHHHhhh* to confirm that you are releasing all your tensions. Take another breath. This time, use the outbreath *AHHHhhh* as a way to let go of all your daily and mundane worries and thoughts. Take a third deep breath in, embracing the sacred in everything that surrounds you. Now, let the third breath out with yet another resounding *AHHHhhh*, as you release the past and open yourself to the *now* moment.

Now, breathe normally, being aware of each breath. As you do this, simply rest in the peace of the moment. When you are ready, reflect on a favorite spiritually awakened person. Do not put limits on the kind of person you "expect" to appear. Remember, this person need not be a saint, but could be a compassionate friend, a dedicated teacher, or a loving family member. Picture this individual in your mind's eye, sitting opposite you, looking at you with his or her loving and knowing gaze.

What principles does he or she embody and hold dear? How do (or did) this person put these into practice? The only thing that separates you is your next action and the commitment to living kindness. Look closely, and you will likely discover that similar principles helped define the lives of everyone from crusaders like Florence Nightingale, Mahatma Gandhi, Martin Luther King, and Mother Teresa to recognized saints and spiritual masters.

Now, switch places with this person. That is, place yourself in his or her beingness, as the person perceives *you* sitting in front of *him or her*. What is it like to see yourself through the eyes of a Buddha or another spiritually adept being? This experience can be overwhelming and humbling at the same time. When you look at yourself through the eyes of this other person, know that you are accepted, appreciated, and loved fully for who you are. Just who you are—nothing more, nothing less, and with the spiritual values you live with right now.

As you watch yourself, why not have the spiritual one you admire send you a kind blessing? Here is a blessing that you can use for this purpose:

> May you light your own spiritual lamp.
> May you experience living kindness in each life moment.
> May you use the principles skillfully, for the benefit of yourself and others.
> May you bring boundless love, compassion, and wisdom into your quest to undertake the spiritual principles.
> May the benefits of these blessings go to all beings.

When you are done, return to your own presence. Rest in the principles of your spiritual model once again. Inquire or ask questions about the principles, and you may gain a new perspective or insight into their deeper meaning. Or you may simply experience the principles in a different way than before. They may even feel more comfortable to you. When you are ready to end your session, take another three deep breaths in and out.

Now, at this point you may find yourself thinking, What if I can't live up to the high standards of these principles? This is too steep a hill to climb. If so, congratulations! You are not alone. Besides, virtues are not meant only for specially gifted and consciously aware persons.

No one is born an all-knowing saint. The Buddha, for example, achieved success only because he learned from his mistakes along the way. Jesus, too, struggled with temptation during his forty days in the wilderness. Part of living kindness is having patience and forgiveness for ourselves when we fall, trip, or stumble along the way. Still, as conscious

beings, our bodies, hearts, voices, minds, and senses possess
the innate ability to tune into these sacred practices.

Principle 1: *Generosity*

We make a living by what we earn.
We make a life by what we give.
—Winston Churchill

It is a wintry morning in the monastery. After meditation ends, all the monks slowly rise and mindfully exit the meditation hall. As we walk into a small hallway, I spy Ashin Thitzana about to enter his room. He is a well-read scholar of Buddhist teachings and one of the youngest monks ever to completely memorize one of Buddhism's three "baskets," or Tripitaka— the three oldest compilations of Buddhist scripture. That is no small accomplishment, considering each basket is several thousands of pages in length. And so, being very curious about his book collection, I ask him if I might take a look.

He nods, and we enter a small, square-shaped room. Next to the door stands a solitary, wood-brown bookshelf. Though it is mostly filled up, I am surprised to find such a modest collection. Nevertheless, I immediately start browsing and scanning the titles, which include books on all religions.

Barely have I begun when he declares, "Choose a book, any book. I would like to give one to you as a gift."

"That's very nice of you," I protest, "but I only want to look."

"I want to be of assistance on your spiritual journey, so please take one," he says.

"I really appreciate your kind offer," I say politely, "but I'm sure these books are very important to you."

"True," he laughs, "I used to be very attached to my books, and there was a time when I couldn't bear to give any of them away."

"Besides, I can always borrow one if I need it," I say, thinking I am off the hook.

"No, I insist, U Vayama," he answers, calling me by my monk's name. "This is part of my spiritual work. Now, I'm giving them away," he says with a kind smile.

For a brief moment I resist. However, during my time with the monks I have learned one thing: Receiving cannot really be separated from giving. The two are like the opposite poles of a magnet connected by an unbroken magnetic field. After all, is it not true that if no one ever received, no one would be able to give? So while I hesitate to take what I know is so precious to this scholar and friend, I am also deeply touched by the purpose and strength of his commitment.

"OK, how about this one?" I say, holding a book that interests me most—one featuring the texts from various schools of Buddhism.

"That's one of my favorite books!" he exclaims without a trace of sarcasm or misgiving. "I'm glad you chose it. May it serve you well, my brother."

"Thank you so much for your help," I reply, looking into brown eyes that glint with delight. At that moment I finally understand where all of this monk's vaunted book collection must have gone! But for me, it is an important lesson about learning to let go of what is most precious, as well as to graciously accept what is given. Saint Francis of Assisi eloquently expresses this idea in his famous prayer:

> For it is in giving that we receive,
> It is in forgiving that we are forgiven.

WHY GIVE?

At first glance, the ancient principle of generosity, known as *dana paramita*, is a simple one. Look more deeply, though, and you will likely discover that this most basic of acts connects us intimately with all physical, emotional, and spiritual elements. Even the Catholic Church, for example, does not choose saints by looking at a candidate's visions or miracles. The gold standard for attaining sainthood is charity. This makes sense when you realize that charity and giving for the well-being of others spring from the seed of love.

Consider this: If not for our mother's "giving" us birth we would not exist. If not for our planet's bounty of food, air, and shelter we would not survive. I am reminded of another wonderful poem by Saint Francis, *Canticle of Brother Sun*, in which he sings the praises of Sir Brother Sun, Sister Moon, Brother Wind, Sister Water, Brother Fire, and Sister Mother Earth, all of which "give sustenance to Your creatures." From this perspective, is not our entire existence based on love? How beautiful, how marvelous to realize that the entire universe must exist because of all that is given—and, ultimately, bound together by love.

Conversely, there are those who look at this same scenario and conclude that our whole existence is based on taking. This has probably been the prevalent view up through the twentieth century. Indeed, some geneticists even believe we possess a "selfish" gene and that without self-interest we would not survive. Looking at our history, it might be hard to argue with them. After all, humanity has been in the grip of what could be termed the "self-interest principle" for several thousands of years. Our very vernacular reinforces the idea that it is a "dog eat dog world," that "nice guys finish last," and that "only the strong survive." Even the complex ideas of scientists such as Charles Darwin are watered down to support the thesis that the law of life is survival of the fittest. Have you ever believed this or thought this on occasion? It would be unusual if you never have.

This self-interest principle is based upon a belief in the separate nature of all things. It supposes an I/you universe competing for limited resources and possessions where when one gains, the other one loses. In truth, Charles Darwin felt that nature was creative and intelligent. He believed that the force of a species' habit or its learning of a behavior could actually affect its heredity. In his book *The Rebirth of Nature*, biologist Rupert Sheldrake tells us that "the notion that the habits of nature evolve under the influence of natural selection is close in spirit to the thinking of Darwin himself, though at variance with the neo-Darwinian doctrines currently predominant in academic biology."[1] Ironically, our very perception that the self-interest principle is a natural law has formed its own habitual pattern of human thought and behavior! Fortunately, however, habits can change.

Of course, there are those who believe that it is completely naïve to give without at least some shred of self-interest. So, how do we respond when someone asks us, "How can you hope to take care of yourself if all you do is give everything away?" We can begin by recognizing that there is an element of truth in what they say.

A SIMPLE TRUTH

If we do not first take care of our own well-being, how will we attend for the well-being of a neighbor? If we do not first love ourselves, how can we begin to know how to love another? If we have no compassion or wisdom for ourselves, what could possibly be available to share with others? If we do not have two pennies in our pocket, how can we lend even a single penny to someone in need? Seen in this way, charity really does begin at home.

This, then, is a simple truth of giving: If we want to give anything away, be it our love, money, time, forgiveness, regrets, sympathy, commitment, blessings, or anything else, we must first manifest it—either from within or materially. It is common in many Buddhist practices, for example, to first bless ourselves, then bless others. Self-interest, then, is not inherently bad. Like with everything else, we just need to find its middle ground. The Dalai Lama confirmed the importance of finding the blessing within when he said, "There is no so-called blessing. The blessing must come within, from one's mental attitude. To expect that blessing from others, it is nonsense."[2]

To make this simple truth most effective, we can do what so many traditions do: practice empowerment. There is the Native American practice, for example, of skipping over the first plant and harvesting the second as a means of honoring Mother Earth by taking only what is needed. Is not this really an empowerment that enables the earth to regive its gifts over and over? Do we not also sustain ourselves when we water a plant, care for a child, commit to any beneficial social action, or help others help themselves?

Enlightened giving and empowerment of others are ultimately in our own best self-interest. The ancient principles show that we are not separate. We need to experience and recognize how giving through empowerment nourishes us all. Perhaps the hallmark of the twenty-first century will be its shift from self-interest to empowerment. But it will only happen when each of us embraces empowerment in thought and deed.

WHAT IS YOUR EMPOWERING GIFT?

It is early morning as I peer through the drizzle looking for an address along Portland's trendy NW 23rd Street. Luckily, I nab a vacant spot right in front of a remodeled Victorian building. To my surprise, I discover that this is exactly where I am to meet Ron Kotkin before he begins his day's work. I climb two long flights of stairs and enter a large room with soothing mist-green walls and white trim. A series of low-backed leather chairs frame the room's perimeter—where Ron takes care of business as a hair stylist.

Ron, however, is not your typical barber. Nearly every day he gives away free haircuts—ranging from 100 to 125 a month—to people who bring in referral vouchers. Most people are sent from homeless shelters, domestic abuse shelters, and foster care centers. Some have drug and alcohol problems, while others are just down on their luck. All need a good haircut, especially when they are going for a job interview. Ron explains that he has been giving away haircuts for more than fourteen years. "I knew how to do something, so I had something to give," he says matter-of-factly, all the while moving nonstop, tidying up his station.

When I ask what prompts him to give charity, Ron stops and faces me. His wiry, energetic frame and brown hair make him look younger than his forty-four years of age. His intense hazel eyes seem to soften as he tells the story of how, years earlier, his young daughter needed speech therapy. Even though he and his wife lacked health coverage, the clinic they visited did not turn them away. Touched by their kindness, Ron responded by offering free haircuts for the clinic's less than well-to-do clients. Soon, other agencies heard about his charity and referred their clients to him.

In walks Mike, a welder who is currently staying at a homeless shelter for men. He hands his voucher to Ron and takes a chair by the sink. After his hair is washed, Mike shuffles over to the barber's chair. I introduce myself, and Mike explains that he is going on an interview later that day. "You got to look good for your job," he says. We talk, and I learn that Mike himself volunteers at the homeless shelter. Obviously, it never occurred to him that just because he needs help, it does not mean he cannot help others.

Ron's next voucher client, a teenager, does not show for his appointment. There are more than 1,500 kids living on the streets of Portland, Ron explains.

Just about then, a dignified looking woman with long-ish, gray-blonde hair enters. Her name is Andrea, and she is a walk-in customer from off the street. But as Ron starts snipping away at her bangs, she reveals that her visit is not accidental. She heard about Ron's charitable ways and wants to support his efforts by being a paying customer.

Together, we talk about what it means to give, and Andrea shares with us that her own granddaughter is disabled. Each Halloween, even though her granddaughter is too sick to go out for "trick or treat," Andrea always helps her dress up for the event. "A lot of burdens in life are too big for families to handle by themselves," she says.

Finally, it is time to leave, and I thank Ron for sharing his story. One thing he has said sticks with me: "I figure if one out of ten people that I work on gives back to the community, then it's worth it to me." From what I have seen, Ron's odds are greater than one in ten. What is more, I realize that our conversations have reached a consensus this morning on one important point:

If everybody did just one thing.

Just one thing. Not even a great thing. Not a world-changing thing, but just one giving thing, just one blessing, just one act of living kindness. The effect of each caring action, no matter how seemingly small, brings blessings into the lives of others. There may be no greater or more important thing that we can do *at this instant.*

And as Ron's example shows, we only need to do what we do best. Each of us possesses a special gift, call it a professional trade, ability, or knowledge that can be beneficial. Maybe you do not have to wait for that perfect charity or volunteer work to come along—perhaps your everyday work can be that work.

If something is stopping you, listen to what it is. Listen with full awareness. You may find that the answer is easier and closer at hand than you could ever imagine.

Experience: *Pay It Forward*

In the movie *Pay It Forward*, directed by Mimi Leder, a young boy comes up with the notion that the world can be changed by taking a good deed, or blessing, and passing it on to others. This is not just a good movie idea. We need to think about how and in what ways we can take our gratitude and pay it forward.

For example, each time you benefit from a blessing, take your sense of gratitude and direct it toward others. You can do this in two simple ways. One, by immediately forwarding any blessing you get by praying that all beings get similar blessings (some monks do this all the time). Or you can perform a similar deed for someone within twenty-four hours. Make a point of letting the recipient know that you do not need to be repaid. Instead, ask the person to send the deed onward to another being. You can even take a vow to "pay it forward," as you will discover in the next principle, effort.

A RAINBOW OF GIVING

We live in a wealth-oriented culture and society. Too often we judge others, and they judge us, by the cars we drive and the jewelry we wear. But as most people who follow that path eventually realize, a possession-centered life does not equate to a fulfilled life. Even a so-called spiritual life can bear the trappings of possession. The first ancient principle is special because it lets us experience our grasping, clinging, and attachments in a myriad of new ways.

The two most fundamental forms for giving consist of conventional, or worldly, giving and transcendent giving. Worldly giving occurs the moment we discriminate or think in real terms about giving. In other words, this form of giving depends upon perceiving all things as objects. The recipient is an object, the giver is an object, and the gift is yet another object. Even if we give selflessly, expecting nothing in return, as long as our giving is subjective, then it is still worldly. Our social and economic systems are based upon this kind of exchange: *I* give *you* some *thing* for which *I* get from *you* some *thing* (or no-*thing*) in return.

In contrast, transcendent giving is when there is no person or object to either give or receive a gift. In fact, there is no gift at all. This is where we go beyond the shores of duality.

This form of giving asks that what is given be surrendered to all beings, without discrimination. Here, giving is as natural, automatic, and necessary to life as breathing. In other words, we give without any attachment whatsoever. Even the object is of no consequence. But how is this possible?

The Bible's Book of Mark (12:29) contains one likely explanation. Here, Jesus' statement to "love your neighbor as yourself" can be interpreted as being about dissolving the walls of separation between people. What really keeps us apart from others, from loving others, and from giving to others? It is our belief that we are separate from them, is it not? If we are actually separate beings, then we need to maintain, support, and protect everything that is tied in with that—our separate being identity, our family identity, our country identity, and so on. But to "love our neighbor as ourself" pierces and transcends that belief in our separateness. It brings us face-to-face with oneness. Here, then, is a clue to the nature and spirit of transcendental giving.

There is an oft-repeated story of how the Buddha, during one of his lifetimes, offered up his body as a meal for a tigress's hungry young cubs. This offering was done as a deed of complete surrender and giving, without a trace of anger or ill will. Even the pain of being eaten piece by piece was accepted with total patience and nonattachment! While this might seem a bit gruesome, the story makes the point that we take nothing material with us when we leave this world, not even our frail, naked bodies.

At the same time, this story gives us hope that we can learn to surrender and accept all that happens to us during our lifetime. Surrender and acceptance, then, are types of giving that we can also experience. This includes surrendering our bodies to old age and disease without sorrow, bitterness, and regret.

While giving can be looked at as either worldly or transcendent, the individual, cultural, and religious expressions of giving are diverse. Yet somehow, like the spectrum of a rainbow, these merge to create one true light. It is from this "rainbow of giving" that we can further experience and express the first principle.

THE GIVEAWAY

One important tradition for many Native American tribes is the ritual "giveaway." It is through the giveaway that they encounter the full richness of giving. Here, giving is not simply viewed as an individual act of generosity, but as a mature period in our lives, a kind of winter season that brings to fruition all we have learned and attained during our journey. The process of giving back what we have taken—such as either materially or through sharing knowledge with others—is like replanting seeds in the soil.

The giveaway acknowledges that there is a time in our lives to repay and give back, just as there is a season in nature for sowing, planting, and harvesting. Even certain animals, such as the buffalo, are considered as "giveaway" animals because they bestow all of their parts, including their flesh, hide, and horns, for the benefit of others.

Which giveaways have graced and benefited your life? Each day, the food on your plate gives away, or surrenders, all its energy to you. Numerous giveaways, from clothing to shelter, keep you warm day and night. From this perspective, is not everything that we use a kind of giveaway? Any of us who feels that we are not getting enough is missing just how much we really are given at each moment.

EIGHT LEVELS OF CHARITY

In Judaism, the concept of giving is essential through what is known as *tzedakah*, or charity. Actually, the roots of the word stand for justice, righteousness, or fairness. It was in the twelfth century that the Jewish philosopher and rabbi Moses Maimonides compiled his "eight levels of charity" as a kind of guide to enlightened giving. The levels, starting from the lowest to highest, are as follows:

1. Giving unwillingly
2. Giving willingly but giving less than you could
3. Giving only after being asked
4. Giving without being asked
5. Giving to a recipient you do not know, but who knows you
6. Giving to a recipient you know, but who does not know you
7. Giving when both parties are anonymous to each other
8. Giving that enables self-reliance

Tzedakah is considered to be one of Judaism's *mitzvahs*, or good deeds. As a mitzvah, charity is not optional, but one of those things that God commands us to do. For that reason, mitzvah is at the heart of Jewish life and tradition. The eight levels of charity are helpful because they let us examine different degrees of openness that we might experience when giving. One ancient Jewish parable from the Talmud teaches about the fairness of tzedakah:

A woodcutter carrying a load of firewood had stopped by the side of the road to rest. When Rabbi Ishmael happened to walk by, the man asked for his help.

"My load is heavy," the woodcutter said. "Would you

mind helping me carry some of my wood?"

"Perhaps I can help in another way," the rabbi answered. "Is your wood for sale? How much do you want for the entire bundle?"

"You may buy it for half a zuz," the woodcutter replied.

"Here," the rabbi said, handing his money to the woodcutter. "Now just leave it where it is. Since the wood belongs to me, I would like to give it to any poor person who needs it to build a fire and keep warm."

"Well, since I am poor," the woodcutter said to the rabbi, "I have the same right as anyone to it. I hereby claim all of this wood for myself."

The man turned to the rabbi and asked a second time, "Would you help me carry my wood?"

Once again, the rabbi handed the woodcutter half a zuz, but this time he declared, "I now proclaim that everyone has the right to this wood—everyone, that is, but you!" With this statement, Rabbi Ishmael showed the woodcutter that good deeds performed out of love for others take precedence over profit or personal gain.[3]

The beauty of giving charity through a mitzvah, or any kind of blessing, is that we never know when the next giving moment will arise. Giving brings us into a state of uncertainty, which is really the *now* moment. If we are so certain of our actions, then they lack spontaneity and freedom, do they not? The rabbi who encountered the woodcutter, for example, could have avoided talking because of fear. He could have been too busy, preoccupied, or insensitive to the woodcutter's situation. Instead, he surrendered to the giving moment, then materialized it into multiple benefits—for the woodcutter and others. This illustrates something about the nature of giving. It is only as present and expansive as our moment-to-moment awareness.

PURIFYING CHARITY

In Islam, giving is recognized as a form of surrender to God's will. It is so vital that *zakat*, a purifying payment or charity, is one of the religion's "five pillars." Traditionally, an annual payment is made for distribution to those in need. Muhammad, the prophet who received the word of the holy Qur'an from God, was himself an orphan who routinely offered food and assistance to the poor. This form of giving is not exclusionary and meant only for other Muslims, but for anyone in need.

For those Muslims who have nothing materially to give, even a smile given to another is an acceptable form of charity. This might prompt us to ask some important questions such as, How many smiles have I given away today? Have I been miserly with my emotions? Have I withheld my caring, my love? Did I spend enough time with those who matter? Did I show compassion and love to myself in trying circumstances?

MISERLY, MARKETPLACE, AND ROYAL GENEROSITY

Some monks in monasteries in Thailand, Burma, and Sri Lanka teach about the "three levels of generosity." A friend of mine who spent about a month living in one such monastery was so impressed by these teachings that he vividly remembers them nearly twenty years later! I like them, too, because, like Judaism's eight levels of charity, they help illumine each of us as to the how, why, who, what, when, and where of giving. The three levels are referred to as miserly, marketplace, and royal generosity.

What is miserly generosity? Like the name implies, it refers to those times when you give less than you know you could—to others or even to yourself. You might experience miserly generosity, for example, when you give away something that you do not really want anyway. Another example of miserly giving is when you give less than you are capable of giving or when you give only because you feel obligated. Or you may be stingy with yourself—holding back from giving yourself some much-needed compassion, love, or even material needs.

Miserly generosity could also take the form of giving someone what *you* think is best for them, not what *they* really want or need. I know of one such case concerning the food donated to a Buddhist monastery where one of the monks suffered from severe allergic reactions to garlic, onions, and other spicy foods. Despite his condition, some who offered food often ignored his requests, either not believing these foods would do him harm or because it was not what *they* wanted to give or cook. Or, perhaps they were not really listening.

None of us is immune to miserly generosity. That is because it is all too easy to bring our own likes, dislikes, and preferences to the table when giving. Being in the giving moment means listening to others with full concentration, not just to our own desires. As miserly generosity illustrates, it is *how* we give that really matters.

What can we do upon discovering that our generosity is miserly? Just being attentive is a good place to begin. There is no need to heap blame or immediately remedy the situation.

Besides, miserly giving is still giving, so that is a good thing! ③What you might want to consider, however, is shining a light into those other areas in your life where you hold on too tightly, where you feel constricted, tight, and rigid. If you have a lot of rules and conditions under which you give, that could be a sign of miserly generosity. Think about how you can loosen the reins and be free to the giving moment—especially toward yourself.

Know, too, that miserly generosity extends beyond gift giving. We can be stingy with our emotions and our love. Withholding a kind word or sentiment. Restrained with our laughter, joy, and spontaneity. Restricted in the sharing of our knowledge and wisdom. Choked up with false pride and the inability to forgive. Do you carry such a burden? If so, let yourself experience what it is like to let it go. You can be the pioneer in your family who gives up the family habit—whether that pattern is about substance addiction, being unforgiving, not asking others for help, or not expressing love. Once you have identified your form of miserly emotional giving, see if you can let it go over the next twenty-four hours. No matter how much any habit or pattern seems to have a hold on you, the future is shaped by the choices you make now. Letting go of your habits just once or simply being more aware for a split moment is a major accomplishment toward giving yourself freedom. You will be that much more unburdened and lighter as a result.

Unlike miserly generosity, marketplace generosity is usually typified by some kind of exchange or expectation. In other words, it is like going to the store. You give something, and you expect to get something in return. It also implies an agreement between two willing parties. What marketplace generosity attempts to do is provide its user with a predetermined, fair, and safe means by which to give and always get something back. Of course, this approach hinders the giving moment because we are always judging, always waiting for the response, for the return on investment.

How can you determine if you are operating under this mode of generosity? One clue might be if you always keep score—comparing what you receive with what you give. The marketplace is usually lurking when giving is an obligation, something that you see as a necessary action. Many of us are torn and conflicted by what we perceive as obligation or responsibility.

How many times have you done something simply because you felt you had to? In this case, the exchange or return for giving might be anything from acceptance from others to respect in the community. You sent that wedding, anniversary, birthday, or business gift out of reciprocation, or because you are the uncle, aunt, or some other relation. The ten ancient principles show us that giving only because of obligation is an empty act. Our giving is also capable of holding love, patience, resoluteness, concentration, effort, virtue, truth, equanimity, and wisdom. The Beatles captured the essence of this idea with their famous phrase "Money can't buy you love."

Then there is the kind of marketplace generosity that happens when you try to control others' behavior or emotions by what you give them or promise to give them. What family has not experienced this kind of conditional giving? While in college I had a friend named Howard, whose parents said they would pay for his tuition only on the condition that he never had a girlfriend. For Howard's father it was a control issue.

After about six months, Howard met someone. When his parents came to visit, he introduced them to his girlfriend and lost his tuition. (Perhaps adversity made him stronger—since he later graduated and happily married that girl!) I am not saying Howard's parents did not have the right to decide what they thought was best for their son. The problem with marketplace, or conditional, giving is that it puts a price tag on everything from love to acceptance. Unfortunately, these price tags often produce resentment.

Yet, even within the context of marketplace generosity, there are alternatives that express a more transcendent kind of giving. Anytime we give with a warm, open heart we make our giving more friendly and compassionate. When we give because we care about the needs of another—regardless of what we might desire or want in return—we are freed from being stuck in the marketplace mentality. With the right kind of effort, our giving can always come from a place of friendship, well-being, and connection to others.

 What is the best you have to give? Think of it as your royal generosity. This is your giving that knows no boundaries. Taken to the limit, it neither discriminates among recipients nor demands anything in return. Joy and love are its divine architects. It is giving for giving's sake, knowing that what we transmit into the universe travels back to the sender. Here, to give and to receive are not separate actions, but parts of the same whole. It is the fruit we eat and the seed we return to the earth.

You will know you are experiencing this kind of generosity when you give unconditionally or anonymously, with no strings attached—when you respond spontaneously should the giving moment unexpectedly arise with friends, family, loved ones, business associates, and even strangers. Royal generosity does not leave you feeling cheated, elated, or superior, but feeling joyful and alive in the giving moment.

This is also a generosity that releases old wounds. It lets you forgive those who may have caused you pain, either intentionally or inadvertently—even if that person happens to be yourself! When you sit in meditation (see "Principle 5: Simplicity and Meditation"), do you not take a break from your many cravings, desires, beliefs, and opinions? By ever so slowly letting go in any number of ways you can experience your own royal generosity.

Royal generosity is not just for the Mother Teresas of the world, it is for real people who struggle with giving on a daily basis. Ultimately, the royal best means bringing your awareness, open heart, unselfish mind, and generosity to each situation as called for. Of course, this does not mean you have to be generous all the time. You still have to take care of your own well-being so you can help others. Truly, this is the first step on the journey to living kindness.

THE GIFT OF GRATITUDE

Outside the window where I work, a stand of Douglas firs stretches tall and upright toward fast-moving white clouds. A shaft of light illuminates a thorny thicket of blackberry bushes. Small bugs wing their way through the sunlight, circling and zipping back and forth. The tender red leaves of a young maple tree flutter in the wind gusts. Watching this, even for a moment, fills me with thanksgiving and awe. A similar experience is available for you as well—right now. Look around. Experience what is there. See the truth. Be grateful for this moment.

We cannot complete our exploration of giving without experiencing gratitude. If all the things we receive are blessings, then to give gratitude is our saving grace. Gordon Hinckley, a Mormon Church leader and author of *Standing for Something*, believes that gratitude is a neglected virtue capable of healing:

Gratitude is a sign of maturity. It is an indication of sin-
cere humility. It is a hallmark of civility. And most of all,
it is a divine principle. I doubt there is anything in which
we more offend the Almighty than in our tendency to
forget His mercies and to be ungrateful for that which
He has given us.[4]

What is your experience of gratitude? Is it something that
you acknowledge and give openly? Or do you parcel it out
with an unwilling heart? Maybe the degree of your gratitude
depends on how, or from whom, you receive your gifts. To be
more aware is the first step in discovering if your gratitude is
miserly, marketplace, or royal.

Sometimes it is awkward to say thank you. There are
many families, and even some cultures, where expressing
gratitude is very difficult. Looking at how your family re-
sponds to gratitude may be a clue to your own attitudes and
feelings. Like saying grace before a meal, gratitude acknowledges that we need others, that we simply cannot do it alone.

Then there is the flip side of the coin: What do you experience when someone does not show gratitude? For example,
I can remember giving gifts and not being thanked. My own
hurt and disappointment at those times let me experience my
own gift-giving expectations and limitations.

Beyond this conditional gratitude, there is thanksgiving
for what is, even when we do not understand or like our circumstances. When we are ill, for example, we can have
gratitude for our bodies telling us that they need our help and
attention. When we are released from that job, we can give
gratitude for being free to move on. Or when we do not receive the congratulations or thanks we think we deserve, we
can just rest in the way things are. When we act wrongly, we
can simply be at peace with our ordinary "as is" perfection.

Gratitude does not have to make anyone feel better. It does not have to fix what is missing. It can just be the experience of what is now.

Experience: *Finding Your Own Giveaway*

Is there an untapped giveaway to be found in your life, in your home, in your heart? This experience can take anywhere from about five to fifteen minutes to complete. It is not meant to be used just this once, but on a daily basis because our giveaways are not as few and limited as you might think.

Before you begin, let us explore the notion of the giveaway from some other perspectives. In the book *A Still Forest Pool*, compiled by Jack Kornfield and Paul Breiter, Thai forest monk Achaan Chah is reported as having said, "When we carry a burden, it's heavy. When there's no one to carry it, there's not a problem in the world."[5] He could be talking about the burden of all our possessions, our desires, our identities, our likes and dislikes, and other things that cause us suffering. These troubles and burdens can weigh us down and make us feel overwhelmed. Conversely, letting them go (en)lightens us.

In another sense, carrying fewer possessions can bring us into harmony with living a simpler, more mindful life. The more possessions we have, the more fearful we become of losing them. Our ancient principle does not ask us to give up all our "stuff." But it does ask us to consider what it means to be caught on the merry-go-round of wanting more and more. As you prepare for this giveaway exercise, it is worth reflecting on the ideas of Mahatma Gandhi, who founded a religious community in India for which nonpossession was a basic principle. He believed that God always gave us what we needed for today, but cautioned about hoarding for tomorrow. Also, consider that the following words from his book *Vows and Observances* were written while he was in prison:

> Possession implies provision for the future. A seeker after truth, a follower of the law of love, cannot hold anything against tomorrow. God never stores for the morrow; he never creates more than what is strictly needed for the moment. If there we repose faith in his providence, we should rest assured that he will give us every day our daily bread.[6]

To begin the exercise, find a quiet place where you can sit down, either on a chair or a meditation cushion. Now, as in the previous chapter's "experience," take a deep breath in. Breathe out, letting out a loud *AHHHhhh* to release all your tensions. Take another inbreath. This time, use the outbreath *AHHHhhh* to let go of all daily and mundane worries. Let your third deep breath embrace the sacred in everything that surrounds you. Now, let this breath out with yet another *AHHHhhh*, as you surrender to the giving moment.

Relive for a moment all the freely given moments that you have experienced and benefited from today. Did the sun give away its glorious sunshine to you? Did the earth give away its fruits and plants for you to eat? Did the trees give away their wood as shelter for the room and furniture you use? Did a family member give away a smile or word of encouragement? Did a neighbor, associate, or stranger give away a mitzvah, or good deed, for you? Did a squirrel, a bird, a gust of wind, or a blossoming flower give away its beauty and essence to you? Take a few moments to visualize all the giveaways that have blessed your life today.

Now, take another breath in, showering yourself in those

giveaways. With your outbreath, let yourself, for the next few minutes, experience the giveaways that you have released and shared throughout the day. Did you make a breakfast give-away for yourself or family? Did you give away your time and energy to a friend who needed someone to talk to? Did you give away a useful suggestion to your employer? Did you give away your love to your family when you first saw them this morning? Did you give away your spot in line to some-one who was older or in need? Did you give away your patience, tolerance, and understanding when someone cut off your car on the freeway?

The final part of this experience involves letting you get in touch with a new giveaway. This is something you could realistically give away within the next twenty-four hours. Again, it could range from an emotional or spiritual giveaway to a material one. Let yourself relax in full attention with the giving moment. Do not force ideas; let them come to you. See what giveaway, or gift, you have to offer.

My wife's grandfather, for example, gave away half of his lunch each day of his life. He would either find someone to give it to or leave it for the birds and critters to eat. Give-aways do more than unburden us. They make us aware of what we can give back, all the time reminding us not to waste the precious gifts that are ours.

Principle 2: *Effort*

The wind is always blowing, but we have to do the work of making our boat seaworthy.

—Eknath Easwaran, *The Mantram Handbook*

A spiritual seeker who was frustrated by his inability to know God approached the nineteenth-century Hindu sage and spiritual leader Ramakrishna. The man explained that he had read scripture and done all the proper things, but still had not found God. In response, Ramakrishna quietly led the man into a river. After they were immersed up to their chests in deep water, the spiritual leader suddenly pushed the man's head under the water. Ramakrishna held the man beneath the surface until he thrashed wildly, struggling for a precious breath.

At the last moment, Ramakrishna lifted him up. The man, sucking in a deep breath, looked at the mystic with shock and alarm. At last, Ramakrishna explained his actions. He told the man that finding God would not be possible until his desire for God was as great as his desire for that life-saving breath of air.

LIGHT YOUR SPIRITUAL LAMP

Effort, or *viriya paramita*, is one principle without which none of the others would be possible. In spiritual pursuits, what appears so easy is often very difficult. That is why effort is such an important tool. For practical reasons, and because engaged and committed effort can make learning anything easier, I have placed the principle of effort after generosity. (The original ordering is generosity, ethics, simplicity, wisdom, effort, patience, truthfulness, steadfastness, loving-kindness, and equanimity. Also, note that the spelling of the paramitas is as used in the ancient Pali texts.)

There is simply no way to get around putting in the effort. For example, I once asked jazz saxophone virtuoso and innovator Eddie Harris how many hours he practiced each day. His answer of "eight hours" explained his special ability to bring an unusual level of joy, spontaneity, and improvisation to his work. Effort and energy give us what we need to be at our best, alert and in the zone, but totally calm at the same time. Even when we are discouraged or exhausted, effort helps us go forward through the daily, skillful application of experience and practice. Of course, we sometimes forget that before effort, we need to have a real enthusiasm, love, or passion for something. Without that, why stick with anything in the first place?

How vital are effort and enthusiasm? So vital that no one—not even a Buddha or an enlightened sage like Ramakrishna—can force or cause another person to change, let alone awaken. Some may be steeped too deeply in pain. Others may be too blinded by pleasure to realize the possibility of or necessity for change. But once you begin the practice of living kindness, you need to learn how to keep the passion of that flame from being blown out in the wind. You need to muster the kind of ongoing effort and discipline that will help it grow ever brighter.

Effort is like a powerful polish and stain remover. It is an indispensable item for your spiritual toolbox because it helps dissolve the rust and corrosion that cover up and dull your ability to experience your uniqueness. Father Thomas Merton, in *New Seeds of Contemplation*, tells us,

> The more a tree is like itself, the more it is like Him. If it tried to be like something else which it was never intended to be, it would be less like God and therefore it would give him less glory. No two created beings are alike. And their individuality is no imperfection. . . . This particular tree will give glory to God by spreading out its roots in the earth and raising its branches into the air and the light in a way that no other tree before or after it ever did or will do.[1]

However, to think it is possible to gain self-knowledge by doing nothing but being your normal self misses the point. You can pour Ajax in the tub and leave it there for days or weeks, but unless you scrub with some real elbow power, nothing gets cleaned.

STORMING THE GATES OF HEAVEN

While effort is useful and beneficial, it is also good to be attentive to the perils of spiritual ambition—those times when the goal threatens to overtake effort. One friend of mine jokes about anyone (including myself) who he believes is trying to "storm the gates of heaven" through intense spiritual practices. I have shared laughs with him over this,

probably because his comment illustrates a common misstep.

So, what is spiritual ambition? I know a woman, Ruth
(not her real name), who went through a painful divorce and
does not want to repeat the suffering that she feels life has
dealt her. She frequently expresses a fervent desire to reach
Nirvana in this lifetime in order to avoid rebirth. It is Ruth's
most urgent goal, one that she orchestrates her entire life
around by taking and organizing meditation retreats.

I am not saying that Ruth's actions do not have many
positive side effects. In her own way, she is building a spiritual community and bringing like-minded people together.
But because she wants spiritual freedom so badly—as a kind
of aversion or escape from suffering—she is actually caught
in yet another web of desire. She craves awakening like a sugar
junkie craves candy. On the contrary, the guiding principles
of living kindness mean breaking free from the roots of desire. Living kindness means finding reality and truth wherever
they happen to be—even in our suffering.

Now, consider the story of the Tibetan *rinpoche* who is
said to have reached enlightenment while buttering a piece of
toast. We can be sure he was not planning his next meditation
retreat at that moment! Not only must he have been fully
present, but all of the rinpoche's accumulated spiritual effort
and discipline laid the groundwork for his awakening. This
story confirms how spiritual wholeness can be found anywhere. And it shows that spiritual ambition does not get us
where we want to go any faster. But it could hinder our
progress.

It is by concentrating our effort on the little steps—right
here, right now—as Buddha says in the *Dhammapada*, that help
us reach our destination:

Are you quiet?
Quieten your body.
Quieten your mind.

By your own efforts
Waken yourself, watch yourself,
And live joyfully.

Master your senses,
What you taste and smell,
What you see, what you hear
In all things be a master
Of what you do and say and think.
Be free.

Follow the truth of the way.
Reflect upon it.
Make it your own.
Live it.
It will always sustain you.[2]

OBSTACLES THAT CHALLENGE EFFORT

As humans, we are, quite literally, balls of energy. The Tibetan Buddhists, for example, believe we comprise several different elements, all energy: earth, water, fire, air, space, and consciousness. The Hindu view is similar, viewing all things as the complex interplay between the three basic *gunas*, or condensed vibratory energies that form the universe. Traditional Chinese medicine looks at health in terms of our *chi* energy. Scientists can quantify our energy output in calories. However we define that energy, what is important is how we use it. Given free rein, our energy can carry us in almost any direction. Or we can train it to get us where we need to go. That is why this principle is essential to spiritual pursuits.

Did you ever go on a roller coaster ride and fall asleep? Or take a doze while mountain climbing? It is doubtful. The novelty and thrill (not to mention the adrenaline rush) probably kept you hyperalert. When it comes to effort and discipline, however, there are various hindrances, or obstacles, that can keep anyone from being attentive.

The main challenges to our effort include the senses and craving, unhealthy emotions, sleepiness and drowsiness, restlessness and anxiety, and doubt. We will need to keep a diligent lookout for these because they can sap our ability to stay focused on our spiritual path and experiences (not to mention all our daily activities).

OVERCOMING CRAVING

Craving and sense desire are powerful enough to disrupt any practice, spiritual or otherwise. Have you ever tried to watch a movie while the person next to you munches on popcorn? If it is not someone who is sharing it with you, your focus on the buttery snack can be disruptive enough to cause you to get out of your seat and visit the concession stand. Cravings can result whenever our "sense desires" strongly attach to anything, such as the smell of popcorn or the image on a magazine cover.

While meditating, for example, the sound of chirping birds might provoke the desire to be outside. The thing about craving is that when we are in that mode we cannot simultaneously concentrate on our practice or apply effort to whatever it is we are doing. Our mind does one thing at a time. That is why this hindrance can also be dangerous if we are operating heavy machinery (a car) or even light machinery (a food processor). So, how can we counteract it?

Just as craving has a beginning, it has an ending. The key to maintaining your effort is to bring your attention to the fact that you have been craving. Simple awareness, recognition, and experience of where you are that moment will end the craving. Of course, it might arise again—even instantly— in which case you need to once again experience its appearance.

Eventually, you may begin to recognize patterns of when your experiencing stops. You can always take the time to investigate the origin of your cravings and desires. It is OK to be a detective, only do not commit yourself to a sentence of lifelong guilt. Guilt and remorse over your cravings are only other hindrances that get in your way and undermine effort.

It does not help when you try to repress or deny your cravings—that will only push the roots of desire underground. Somewhere, somehow, they will reappear elsewhere in your garden of thought. The best antidote for reducing craving in your life and spiritual practices comes from an awakened experience and acknowledgment of the craving itself.

OVERCOMING UNHEALTHY EMOTIONS

The obstacle of unhealthy emotions can affect even the most devoted spiritual work. Suppose you just had an argument with your spouse, boss, friend, or neighbor. If you carry negative emotions around with you—such as anger, frustration, disappointment, impatience, fear, hatred, resentment, lust, greed, envy, and sorrow—then the calmness and openness necessary for your experience of the principles will evaporate.

Almost anything, even your own effort, can cause unhealthy emotions to arise. A ringing telephone or other external
interruption—as well as your own lack of fulfillment with your
spiritual experiences—could cause you to feel uninspired, frustrated, bored, or angry. Do not be surprised if this happens to
you on the road to living kindness. No one is exempt from
this hindrance of emotion, not even the most experienced and
committed persons.

When you recognize unhealthy emotions, give yourself
permission to let them go. Try to recognize their origin. Then,
find the gentle, quiet, peaceful center within you. This way
you can use your effort to stay in the present moment.

OVERCOMING SLEEPINESS

③   Then there is the obstacle of sleepiness, which may seem
innocuous, but can shut off your engine of effort very quickly.
You may actually be physically tired, or a thought may lead
you to become drowsy or feel lazy. Maybe there is an unpleas-
ant chore or other activity that you would rather avoid. Or
perhaps you have simply gotten into the habit of shutting
down or sleeping if you do not have a defined task.

Whatever the cause, you first need to experience and note
the condition of your sleepiness. This could be as simple as
repeating the word *sleepy* once or twice. Sometimes, this may
be sufficient enough to eliminate your drowsiness. You can
also try to identify the thought that caused you to become
drowsy and lose energy.

If neither of these works, then you need to pump more
heat and energy into your system. In this case, take a deep
breath. Hold it for at least eight seconds before exhaling. Do

this as many times as necessary until you feel yourself becoming more awake and alert. Do not be surprised if you feel a burst of energy. When you have finished deep breathing, you can resume your normal breathing and focus your effort.

OVERCOMING RESTLESSNESS

(4) Restlessness or anxiety is almost the opposite condition of drowsiness. When you are restless, anxious, or worried, the mind and body are just too active to apply consistent, directed effort and discipline.

As a writer, for example, I have experienced restlessness more than once. I have noticed that after intensive writing periods my mind is still attached to the world of thoughts and ideas. Sometimes it feels as if my thoughts were moving a thousand miles an hour. Or I could be thinking about my next work session. When I recognize and experience my distractedness (which is not hard), I often note the word *restless* or *anxious* to myself. If that does not work, then slow, deep breathing is another antidote for this condition. Deep breathing brings the body into focus and helps ground our effort in the physical world. After we become aware that our mind has calmed down, we can resume our normal awakened effort.

OVERCOMING DOUBT

(5) Doubt may be the last obstacle to effort, but it is not the least of them. In fact, its influence may be enough to erode effort in many aspects of life. At some point in your experience and discipline you will undergo doubt. Is this practice any good? Is my effort really paying off? How do I know I can

trust my path, teacher, teachings, book, vow, rules, the community—fill in the blank—and so on? Through your doubt
you probably raised some good questions. So how can you
dispel or answer your doubt, or keep it from diminishing your
hard effort and ability to experience the ancient principles?

(1) One way to deal with doubt is to just notice it. Experience it. What does it feel like? Where is it coming from? As
before, simply repeat the word *doubt* or *doubting*. There is nothing wrong with doubting. One of the best examples is Saint
Thomas—the original "doubting Thomas" who doubted Jesus'
resurrection. Not only did he go forward to exemplify great
faith, but some historians believe he brought Christianity to
India in the first century A.D.

(2) Another way to answer doubt is to continue looking for
answers. Recognize that you are still learning. Talk with others who are knowledgeable. Seek answers elsewhere. No one
expects you to take these principles at face value without questioning and experiencing them firsthand. Personally, I answer
my questioning through knowledgeable friends, teachers, and
a variety of different translations of spiritual works and sacred texts. I can even go on the Internet to look for resources
worldwide. We are blessed with all the tools we need to overcome obstructions to effort and our path.

Trekking any spiritual path is a balancing act. As you
gain effort and mastery, you also gain ease. That means that
while you may work harder, the effort will come more naturally. While you will certainly encounter new
distractions—and who does not—you also have the means to
overcome them. Do not be discouraged. There is always a new
moment in which to experience living kindness.

SIMPLY FOLLOW YOUR VOWS

Overcoming hindrances to effort will help keep your spiritual lamp lit. But when it comes to feeding the flame, you will want to engage discipline, commitment, perseverance, and passion. This is where vows can make a difference.

As you may know, monks and nuns from many religious orders often take new names when they are ordained—a symbol of inner rebirth and renewal through a more spiritually meaningful word. The name given to me while a monk, U Vayama, was a constant reminder of the need to apply myself and challenge spiritual complacency. The name means "right effort," and I must admit I have always wondered if the senior monks who decided upon my name were trying to send me a message. If so, it worked!

After I put on those saffron robes, I can tell you that there was no more spiritual window-shopping for me. I had made my purchase, so to speak. That is not to say that I did not experience some buyer's remorse. I can still recall the first time I went to my room with two other new monks—both obviously more comfortable than I was.

Sitting down, swathed in my robes, head freshly shaven, I wondered if I had not somehow betrayed my birth religion. I wondered a lot of things until, finally, I decided to make it all part of my work. Sitting in meditation was painful, so I used the pain. I watched it, like everything else, come and go. I watched my uneven breath, my aching knees, my senses, my consciousness, my random creativity, my drowsiness upon awaking at four o'clock in the morning, my unhappiness at certain rules, even my nondesires. It was not magic that I was suddenly able to bring my undisciplined mind and body to the work before me. I simply followed my vows.

SACRED VOWS TO NOURISH THE SPIRIT

Taking a vow can be scary. What if you fail to keep it? What if you decide it is wrong for you at some later time? What is the difference between a vow and a commitment? Do we need either for spiritual growth and practicing the ancient principles? All these questions are worth exploring.

For example, you may have a committed relationship with your partner. You may even sit down in private with each other and discuss how committed you are. But as married spouses you go a step further. You take a verbal vow in public with witnesses—as well as a written one—to uphold certain principles and values with relation to one another. How you manage to keep your end of the vow depends on the constant application of self-discipline and good judgment.

Some people believe that self-discipline is limiting and lacking in freedom. But what good is freedom that exposes us to behaviors, choices, and lifestyles that adversely affect our health and happiness? If, for example, I give myself the freedom to use drugs, then I risk bodily and mental health that truly limit my future. Actually, we have greater freedom when we lead a simpler, healthier life. While discipline may cause us to sacrifice some short-term pleasure, it will also help us gain some long-term, enduring benefits for mind, body, and spirit. So, which offers greater freedom?

As is written in *Notes from the Unstruck Music from the Gayan of Inayat Khan*:

The path of freedom
Does not lead to the goal of freedom;
It is the path of discipline
which leads to the goal of liberty.[3]

A vow is like a very specific, formalized commitment. Taking a vow means that you set a powerful intention to think and act in a definitive way. Holding a vow is not to be taken lightly. The right vows can put you on a direct path toward attaining your spiritual goals, and their purpose is to guard against temptations and dangers that can cause you to lose your way.

Commitment alone, on the other hand, does not offer the same strength and sticking power as a vow. That does not mean it is not useful. Certainly, you can obtain benefit from spiritual work that is done with no commitment or with a lot of commitment. But you may find that the obstacles are harder to overcome without a vow.

In his book *The Dharma*, Tibetan Kalu Rinpoche contrasts the differences between a vow and a commitment:

> Suppose there are two houses filled with identical trea-
> sure, exactly the same, except that one has a single door
> which is firmly bolted, and the other has many doors, all
> wide open. The house with the one door firmly bolted is
> in little danger of thieves, but the house with many doors
> is always in danger of losing its precious contents. This
> is the difference between someone who has a formal dis-
> cipline and lives up to it and someone who has not.
> Commitment to discipline . . . [through vows] gives the
> means to guard against faults and the loss of the benefits
> of Dharma practice. Without this formal commitment, one
> must have great diligence and intelligence, since the dan-
> ger that mistakes will occur and benefits be lost is always
> present.[4]

There is nothing wrong with being emotional or nervous about taking vows for the first time—not to mention the

second and third times, and so on. That only means that you
take your vows seriously. Remember, however, that any spiritual commitment you make should benefit yourself and others.
Do not take a vow simply because it is required for a particular path or because someone else thinks it is worthwhile. It is
you, your heart, and your passion that make a vow worthwhile, not the other way around.

Experience: *Making Your Vow Work*

Spiritual vows that generate effort do not have to be complex and ritualistic. They can be simple, like taking a personal
vow to meditate each day. If you are new to spiritual vows,
begin with one that is easy. I know of a woman, for example,
who benefited from meditation but could not seem to find the
time to meditate regularly. When I suggested she take a vow,
she resisted. Her attitude changed when I said she could begin with a short vow—such as meditating for five minutes
each day for one month. She successfully completed that vow
and lengthened her vow as time went on.

Now, think about what level of commitment you are willing to make toward your spiritual work, even with regard to
the material in this book. No one knows better than you do
what kind of intensity you can handle. Whatever you decide,
stick with it. It could be a vow to read this entire book, to add
other books to your reading list, or to do all of the experiences
in each chapter. What matters most is that you fulfill the commitment to yourself. I think you will be glad that you did.
Not only will you gain additional spiritual strength, but you
will find that your commitment grows as time goes on.

What happens after a vow? Begin by setting aside the
time to fulfill your vow. Work on a plan that includes when

and where you will practice. Take it day by day. Try to be mindful of your vow throughout the day. If necessary, find time to practice by waking up a little earlier in the morning or going to sleep a little later at night.

No one expects you to be mindful of the ten guiding principles twenty-four hours a day—and I would not pretend that I am. And, yes, there may be times you fall short of your objectives. But that does not make you (or the vow) a failure. You can forgive yourself, then search for other ways to better understand, experience, and keep the vow.

One good way to maintain a vow is to take it in the presence of others. This gives you added strength because you can depend on like-minded seekers to support and encourage your effort. Stay in contact with one or more of them, or arrange meetings where you and others can practice together.

Sacred vows are not intended only for the spiritually adept. They are important tools for each and every one of us to use. If you feel that a vow will strengthen your commitment and effort, then there are many from which to choose. These may include more traditional ones made before a spiritual community or teacher, vows taken in the name of a spiritual being like Buddha or Jesus, and those that you can take to heart for yourself.

GOING FOR REFUGE

One well-known Buddhist vow is called "Going for Refuge." The idea of taking refuge implies that the conditions around us are stormy and difficult. Whenever we take this vow, we feel a sense of security and protection. This vow anchors our commitment and assures us that we are not alone in our quest. Within this context, one typically vows to take refuge in the teacher (the Buddha), the teachings (the Dharma), and the spiritual community (the Sangha).

Taking refuge is open to all seekers, regardless of their beliefs. This is especially true when we consider that we can trust in the timeless wisdom and truth embodied by our own faiths' spiritual teachers—be it Buddha, Jesus Christ, Vivekananda, or others. For many, though, the idea of taking refuge in a teacher or guru raises some important questions and side issues worth discussing. Does this mean that all spiritual teachers embody the qualities of awakened enlightenment? Does a teacher need to be enlightened? Do we even need a guiding teacher?

Much has been made of finding the right guru, or spiritual teacher, who initiates and leads students into spiritual work. The two syllables from which the word *guru* is derived mean the removal (*ru*) of darkness (*gu*). This darkness can be thought of as ignorance of the spirit, the mind, and the heart. The guru, then, dispels ignorance by shining the light of truth. So while a teacher can embody the truth, the same potentiality exists in all of us.

There is also a self-contained guru principle that operates within each individual. In his book *Healing Mantras*, Thomas Ashley-Farrand writes, "The true guru is not some person to whom you give complete and slavish obedience. The true guru is a principle that resides in your own heart. . . . In Sanskrit, this guru principle is called the *upaguru*, or 'teacher without form.'"[5] So in the ultimate sense you can serve as your own guru, the finder of light and truth in your heart.

This is not to discourage you from seeking a wise and compassionate teacher. Consider, for example, how teachers can answer specific nagging questions that books and other sources sometimes cannot. I have been fortunate to be assisted by more than one wise guide. But you have to accept that all teachers are human and subject to frailty. That is why I always come back to the Buddha's own refrain, "Be a lamp unto yourself." Take refuge in the embodiment of the truth and learn what you can from others who are wiser than you are. And even if you take a guru, follow your heart to make sure that it feels right. In the end, you are still your own guru.

Likewise, we take refuge in the Dharma, or the teachings that speak to us, because we can realize and express the teachings in our daily actions and behavior. And, whatever our faith, taking refuge in the Sangha helps us associate with those who bring a greater dimension to our quest for living an awakened life. But the Sangha is not just those who pray, study, or practice with us. It is much more.

First, the Sangha is not exclusive or restrictive, as some like to think. It is not about "my" Sangha, but about all those who are truth seekers, regardless of their religious belief system. In Tibet, for example, there is only "the" Sangha, which includes all persons who support our efforts to awaken. Naturally, then, a vow to take refuge in the Sangha also means finding the right people to associate with on a daily basis. This does not mean we ignore and shun those who think differently. But if others are truly counterproductive to helping us stay on the path, then we have to question how our association with them benefits or serves.

Yet, as you take refuge in the community, you can also reflect on how all persons are interdependent, regardless of country of origin, race, creed, or belief. Some spiritual leaders even go so far as to say the Sangha contains all those in our communities, including family, friends, coworkers, partners, teachers, students, and all those with whom we interact. Certainly, there is some truth here. After all, do we not all breathe the same air, all share the resources of our planet, and all have the same basic needs to be met? This extended Sangha is illustrated by the monk who greeted all who knocked on the door with the words "The Lord is at the door." He recognized the divine in each being.

Before meditation, or other spiritual practices, you can repeat the following words out loud or silently. If you want, you can place your palms together at your heart center. This can be a personal vow, and you do not need any witnesses to make it meaningful.

> I take refuge in the Buddha [the Lord, etc.],
> I take refuge in the teachings,
> I take refuge in the community.

VOWS OF PRAYER

Prayer is an excellent way to express a vow. Through prayer you can open your heart and gain greater faith. When you commit to prayer, you set an intention just as with a vow. And as with vows, prayers work best when repeated or reflected upon daily. In this way, they go deeper and deeper into all levels of consciousness.

Whatever prayer you choose—and there are excellent ones from all traditions—make a point of saying it for at least forty days in a row. You may also want to set an intention for the prayer to help reveal for you some new meaning in one or more of the ancient principles. One Bible prayer (1 Chron. 4:10) that helps build the courage and strength necessary to stay on the path is the Jabez prayer: "And Jabez called on the God of Israel, saying, 'Oh, that you would bless me indeed, and enlarge my territory, that your hand would be with me, and that you would keep me from evil, that I may not cause pain.' So God granted him what he requested."

Here is another prayer you can repeat as you experience the principles. Feel free to adapt this, and others, to suit your sensibilities.

May all my vows be filled with joy and love.
May my discipline offer up fruits of awakening and
    liberation.

BODHISATTVA VOW

The "Bodhisattva Vow" represents a commitment to practice the ancient principles. Not surprisingly, different teachings emphasize slightly modified sets of principles, or perfections. The Buddha's ten guiding principles are found in early Buddhist teachings. And although generosity, effort, patience, ethics, simplicity and meditation, and wisdom are common to all teachings, the Mahayana and Tibetan traditions sometimes substitute four others.

What are we to make of this? Are some lists right, while others are wrong? I like to think it means that we can appreciate the differences. Over time, new perspectives and interpretations always keep emerging. All are capable of helping us gain self-knowledge and understanding. We can learn from them all. Besides, it is not the lists that are important, but the work and experience that these and other values offer us.

Here is one particularly moving Japanese Zen form of the Bodhisattva Vow, as translated by Lama Surya Das:

Sentient beings are numberless: I vow to liberate them.
Delusions are inexhaustible: I vow to transcend them.
Dharma teachings are boundless: I vow to master them.

The Buddha's enlightened way is unsurpassable: I vow
to embody it.[6]

This vow, or any other, can be chanted daily—before your
practice, when you awaken each morning, or when you go to
bed at night. Still, you do not have to take this vow to fully
experience the Buddha's ancient principles. Use only those
vows that both feel comfortable and immerse you in the sacred center of your being.

Experience: *Seeking an Effort-Charged Name*

The belief that sound and name are inseparable from our
spiritual nature has existed for thousands of years. Ancient
Egyptians believed that their souls could reach the kingdom
of the afterworld only by knowing the names of those
gatekeepers who guarded its doors. Even today, Native American Zuni Indians express "spirit" by the wind and the breath.
Eskimos believe that a person's name, soul, and body are forever intertwined. Since new names represent inner rebirth and
renewal, why not give yourself a new, spiritually meaningful
and energizing name? Let this name recharge you with greater
effort and discipline.

You do not have to tell anyone your new name; you can
keep it your personal secret if you want. Or you can ask those
in your spiritual community to address you by this new name.
Let them know what inspired you to choose it. You could even
ask for input for a spiritual name from a teacher or friend.

Get a pad of paper and write down all the names that
come to mind. Your spiritual name could be a salutation like
"Namaste," or "Shalom." Or it could be a cosmic sound such
as *"om."* Another suggestion is to write down the names of

spiritual heroes, like Gandhi or Mother Teresa. You can also imagine yourself as the embodiment of a sage or spiritual leader, in which case a name would be superfluous.

You could also find a quality or principle that you feel would give you strength. As I mentioned earlier, the name U Vayama, or "Right Effort," helped push me beyond my tendency for spiritual laziness. If you find one that is right for you, keep it. If not, continue searching. Have faith that by putting in the effort, the right name will appear.

Principle 3: *Patience*

Straight up from this road
Away from the fitted particles of frost
Coating the hull of each chick pea,
And the stiff archer bug making its way
In the morning dark, toe hair by toe hair,
Up the stem of the trillium,
Straight up through the sky above this road right now,
The galaxies of the Cygnus A cluster
Are colliding with each other in a massive swarm
Of interpenetrating and exploding catastrophes.
I try to remember that.

—Pattiann Rogers, *Firekeeper*

An ancient story from the Jewish Talmud tells about the time
two men made a bet whether Hillel, a wise and famous rabbi,
could be made to lose his patience. One of the men waited

until late Friday—the sacred Sabbath night—and interrupted Hillel as he prepared for his day of rest. Three times the man knocked at Hillel's door, and each time he asked a silly, if not trivial, question. And yet each time, Hillel respected both the questioner and the question with a worthy answer. This was just too much for the man to bear, and at last he blurted out that Hillel's patience had just cost him a large sum of money. Again, the rabbi calmly answered that the value of patience was worth much, much more than any worldly sum.

THE ROOTS OF IMPATIENCE

The principle of patience and forbearance, or *khanti paramita*, seems to be one of the least cultivated in our comparison-oriented, quick-serve culture. Over the past few years, our lifestyle has become dependent on fast food, one-hour photo development, and same-day cleaners, to name a few. Why is it that we are so impatient about our time—perhaps *obsessed* or *controlled* are better terms—that we have begun to differentiate between "quality" time and other time? And when we have to wait in a long line—for tickets or at the bank—why do we so easily become anxious and critical? Why do we fill ourselves up by counting the moments saved instead of being *fulfilled* by the moments lived?

If we are to understand patience and forbearance, we need to understand the roots of impatience and harsh criticism. At some time or another, have we not all been faced with the kind of criticism or events that prod us to react—either with anger or otherwise? No human being, not even a king, a president, or a Buddha, can escape such trying circumstances. There was a time, for example, when the Buddha and his monks were the target of unkind rumors while staying in a particular village. This made it especially difficult for the monks to get enough food to eat from community offerings. The Buddha's cousin and trusted aid Ananda exhorted the Buddha to leave and seek a town more to their liking. The Buddha refused the request, saying,

> No, Ananda, there will be no end in that way. We had better remain here and bear the abuse patiently until it ceases and then move on to another place. There are profit and loss, slander and honor, praise and blame, pain and pleasure in this world; the Enlightened One is not controlled by these external things; they will cease as quickly as they come.[1]

Impatience comes from our reaction to something *outside of* ourselves, does it not? We are unhappy, hurt, or dissatisfied with something, and so we become impatient. Or perhaps our personal expectations are not met, and so we measure the difference with harsh words, thoughts, and actions. Sometimes, this impatience is directed toward ourselves. In truth, the roots of impatience can be found within our own unease with things as they are! We just cannot absorb or accept the fact that x, y, or z is not like we want or expect it to be.

Now, you may be asking, "What is wrong with being frustrated when things take too long or when someone breaks a promise?" I am not saying you should turn off your feelings. This ancient principle of patience can help us feel our emotions—but without having to pay a price that ends up hurting ourselves or others. Too often, our impatience and unease with the way things are, are simply excuses for anger or criticism directed at others. Many of us grow up in families teeming with anger. This is not to say that we should not feel anger and frustration from time to time. However, while anger and criticism may be effective short-term strategies for correcting certain situations, they are highly ineffective and destructive in the long term—both in business and personal relationships.

Think for a moment about a relationship you cherish. The chances are this relationship has been cultivated over time. Friendship grows in a field nurtured with care, encouragement, love, wisdom, forbearance, patience, freedom, honesty, tolerance, and generosity. On the other hand, it withers when fed a steady diet of criticism, doubt, control, discouragement, envy, jealousy, dishonesty, and greed. All of these poisons are the obstacles to patience. For example, if I try to save time at someone else's expense—such as cutting in line— then I confront the obstacle of being greedy with regard to time. The fact that we encounter such obstacles each day is not a bad thing—for without them, we would not learn patience!

The cost of impatience, however, goes far beyond our relationships with others. It can even severely diminish our own health and well-being. Have you ever had personal expectations that went unmet or unfulfilled? Did you fail to achieve some important goal? What did that feel like? Blame and criticism heaped upon oneself can be damaging in many physical ways—including depression, anxiety attacks, ulcers, migraines, and heart disease, to name a few. If you ever thought that impatience was not a big deal, think again!

I can remember, for example, the feeling I had after getting my scores on a college entrance exam. Prior to the exam I had been unable to rest or prepare adequately. Right away, I blamed myself for the score, thinking it would ruin my chances for acceptance. Then something happened. I realized that a test could not measure *me*. After all, there were other criteria for admission, and I decided to not focus solely on the test.

Instead, I let it go. At the same time, I let go of my feelings of blame, guilt, and inadequacy. This also released me from the weight of my expectations or desired outcome, so I could return to my present-moment blessings.

Patience and forbearance help us to let go of a desire, as well as the burden that comes with it. To experience this ancient value is to open the doorway to greater self-knowledge and freedom. As the *Tao Te Ching* counsels,

> The world is won by refraining.
> As I refrain, the people will reform;
> Since I like quiet, they will keep order;
> When I forebear, the people will prosper;
> When I want nothing, they will be honest.[2]

TRANSFORM AND ABSORB

Experiencing patience is about more than just overcoming external obstacles that face us daily. At a deeper level, it is about transforming them. It is about being big enough to absorb them, like the earth absorbs the rain or the air absorbs the warmth of the sun. Nature knows how to wait. Through storm, wind, fire, rain, squall, or earthquake, there is not a grumble of discontent. Not a criticism of how things ought to be. Not a measurement comparing one external event to another. Things happen at a pace beyond human knowing and beyond the human convention of time. There is no expectation, no desire for things to be one way or the other.

Is it possible to view the actions of others, even hurtful actions, with greater understanding and impartiality? This presents a great challenge to our persona, or ego identity. Santideva, an eighth-century Buddhist-Indian mystic and monk, tells us in the classic *A Guide to the Bodhisattva Way of Life* that reacting to the unkind behavior of others "is inappropriate as it would be toward a fire, which has the nature of burning."[3]

To accomplish this kind of impartial patience requires all the ancient principles. You could, for example, imagine yourself to be a vessel of water, one that is large enough to absorb and dilute the suffering of others. The larger and more understanding your vessel, the less you will feel impacted by the sufferings that are poured in your direction. Remember, however, that you cannot be stained or harmed by opening up to suffering that exists. Yet you can help to transform it through patience, love, and the other ancient values.

Again, it is Santideva who gives us an important key to generating this kind of transformation: "When fire spreads from one burning house to another, one should bundle up the straw and the like, take it out, and discard it. Likewise, when the mind burns with the fires of hatred due to attachment, one should immediately cast it aside."[4]

Is there a straw inside of you that threatens to catch fire? I once worked with a perfectionist, Ben (not his real name), who was so critical that he blamed others when things did not go as planned. Part of the problem was that he was always telling people how to do their jobs. Ben's inner critic ignited each strand of straw. It is only by experiencing and becoming more aware that you can discard the fire-burning straw that is in your life.

Experience: *Letting Impatience Go*

In a culture that emphasizes that "fast is a measurement of good," the obstacles to patience can easily become a mental habit. We get addicted to doing things faster, criticizing others, staying in control, and so on. For this experience, you will try to become more aware of your moments of impatience. Even as you are reading this, do you find yourself scanning ahead to get to the actual experience? If so, then good for you! Each time you become more aware of your impatience to people or situations, the more you can learn to let go of your expectations.

This is a simple exercise. It is all about recognizing your impatience and then letting it go with a long, deep breath. Right now—or each morning—state the affirmation:

May I be more aware of my impatience throughout the day.
May I observe it and experience it, without judgment.

Now, let yourself become more attuned to those moments when you feel tense, upset, angry, nervous, or impatient. What is happening externally that is causing this reaction? If you can, ask yourself, "What expectation am I holding onto at this moment?" If you cannot quite figure it out right then, that is all right. What is important is that you take a deep, long breath in. Hold it for several beats, then let it go. As you exhale the breath, *feel yourself letting go of your expectations and impatience.* If you still feel impatient, take another breath and release it again. Repeat this until you feel the precious moment presented to you.

Now, think about the way things really are—not the way you want them to be. Can you find a way to imagine a vessel large enough to hold this situation or circumstance? What if it were a storm, tornado, or other natural disaster? Keep in mind, too, that even the worst hurricanes or volcanic eruptions do not last forever. Patience is not just about being gentle to others. It is about being kind, gentle, and compassionate toward

ourselves. If we do not have an ounce of patience for ourselves, how can we possibly give it to others?

EXTREME FORBEARANCE

Nobody is perfect. And so we have to deal with the difficulties, quirks, and idiosyncrasies of others. It is all too easy
to condemn and criticize other people. This is especially true
when we live and work in close quarters with another—be it
a relative, spouse, friend, or coworker. Forbearance has little
in common with holding your tongue out of the fear of reper-
cussion or reprisal. Forbearance is not about quietly holding
onto a grudge. Neither is it about being codependent and per-
mitting abuse. On the contrary, to forbear means accepting
criticisms with grace—even when one is justly or unjustly re-

nounced, abused, and reprimanded. The act of forbearance
requires wisdom and can serve as a powerful gesture of compassion and love.

Do not fear that you are treading this path alone, however. There are some wonderful examples that guide us in the
merits of forbearance. Throughout his life, Jesus demonstrated
the power of forbearance to those around him; his example
has become an important part of Christian thought and living. For example, Saint Paul (Gal. 6:2) instructs us to "carry
each other's burdens, and in this way you will fulfill the law
of Christ." He also tells us (Rom. 14:12–13), "So then, each of
us will give an account of himself to God. Therefore let us
stop passing judgment on one another."

The emphasis on forbearance has also allowed the members of monastic communities to exist in harmony, peace, and
unity. Simply because someone is a member of a particular
group does not ensure harmony. In his *Rule of St. Benedict*—

wise guidelines for truth seekers living together—the sixth-century monk Saint Benedict made a point of urging all monks to be "supporting with the greatest patience of one another's weaknesses of body or behavior, and earnestly competing in obedience to one another."[5] This tradition continues today.

Forbearance, then, acts as a sacred thread that strengthens the bond to others. It asks us to go beyond our own limited personal viewpoints and hold the burdens of others without judgment—and with tolerance for our differences. It brings goodhearted gentleness into our relations and associations. It helps us to accept difficult circumstances and suffering without imposing expectations. And it encourages us to develop our nonreactive, transforming, and expansive capabilities.

Can you think of an example from your own life where someone gave you the gift of extreme forbearance? Not too long ago I got an e-mail from my friend Jim, who was looking for a set of cassette tapes that he had loaned someone and now needed. Jim sent the e-mail to several people because he could not remember to whom he had given the tapes. When I saw the e-mail I was crestfallen and embarrassed. Although I prided myself on returning books and other items, I had moved out of state and the tapes moved with me! Instead of coming up with excuses I immediately called Jim on the phone and said I had the tapes. He explained why he needed them, without so much as a vowel of blame or criticism about why I had never returned them. I mailed them out to him that day, grateful for what I personally consider an important lesson on how living kindness comes with extreme forbearance.

Consider, also, that there can be forbearance toward your own body. Do you ever push your body too hard? Do you ask it to keep going even when it is exhausted? Do you keep it awake when it begs for sleep? Hindus, for example, believe that the body is the temple of the divine spirit—even food is thought to be a condensed energy source that mixes with our spirit. The wrong foods can cause sloth or increased desire, while the proper ones help our spiritual growth. Be patient and forbearing to the needs of your body, and it just might take you a long, long way.

What would it be like to experience a single day of extreme forbearance? How do you know if you might have a need to cultivate it? One way is to ask, How comfortable am I not speaking? If you feel a compulsion to share your thoughts, to convince others of your point of view, or to interrupt others in midsentence, then you may want to become more attuned to this guiding value. Another clue might be to examine your family pattern. Many of us grew up in families where forbearance was practically nonexistent. If getting in the last word or being right was or is a sign of victory in your family, then forbearance will offer you a new perspective. And I assure you, it is a useful one.

SEEKING DIALOGUE

Often, we are taught that in order to become successful it is necessary to be persuasive. Leaders mesmerize us with their inspiring words. Celebrity talk shows feature glib and witty guests. We argue and debate instead of sharing thoughts. The problem, however, is that as soon as we fall in love with what we say and how we sound, we stop listening. We even forget the value of not speaking at all. Forbearance, and extreme forbearance, makes space to listen without judgment—without resorting to snap decisions about "right" and "wrong."

We can think of how we use communication as being on a continuum. At one end is a position of absolute certainty, righteousness, and a singular point of view—even though that view may be held by many others. This polarity uses words as a verbal hammer, to pound its viewpoint into another. Here, communication allows no space for other perspectives, no space for mutual discussion, exploration, and growth. Needless to say, to be on the receiving end of this kind of communication can be agonizing. Those who communicate in this style may not even be aware of it.

At the other end of the continuum is dialogue, the process of a mutual search for truth and understanding. Dialogue cannot be practiced without forbearance and listening fully. The strength of dialogue is its recognition that truth resides amid our shared knowledge. In his book *On Dialogue*, physicist David Bohm writes, "It is clear that if we are to live in harmony with ourselves and with nature, we need to be able to communicate freely in a creative movement in which no one permanently holds to or otherwise defends his own ideas."[6]

Through the art of dialogue, living kindness gently carries us beyond our limited perspective. Though it may be difficult, the potential for forbearance and dialogue is always present. You can start by shifting away from your limited perspective, even for a minute at a time. Give yourself and others the gift of extreme forbearance. Let others say what they will, without argument. Be still, so the sounds of silence can blow through and around you. Watch and listen to the actions and words of those around you like you would the ocean's waves. Pay attention to how some waves are larger and more ominous, while others foam gently into the sand.

As others speak let yourself listen. Listen not only to the words, but what is beneath the voice. Bring a sense of tolerance to the suffering and pain that overflows in others. See if you can hold it in your heart, without condemnation or blame. When you want to talk, let yourself remain silent. Listen to your inner voice, too. When it criticizes, do not answer. Simply watch and observe it.

Eventually, you can engage others in dialogue by asking questions and, always, by listening. You may discover that a whole new kind of communication springs up. What was once frozen and stilted can become a more free, lively, and meaningful communication. Take your time as you explore how to let forbearance and dialogue into your life. When you find dialogue or forbearance difficult, take a deep breath and let go of your discomfort, your expectations, your opinions, your desires. Let go of the burden! Is not life lighter without it?

If, at times, you are unable to practice extreme forbearance, simply be aware of your experience of impatience. Then try again. Do not heap blame on yourself when you stumble. With the ancient principles there is no failure. Walking this path brings only experiencing, trying, and awakening. Eventually, you will become more adept at this guiding principle.

FEEL THE RESISTANCE

As you experience patience and forbearance, you will probably confront some inner resistance. You may feel irritation at the notion of waiting patiently in line. Or maybe you will be tied in knots as you let your spouse or someone else have the last word. Or perhaps the only way you will forbear criticism will be by leaving the room! Whatever your particular situation, do your best to become aware of your resistance. There is nothing really surprising about resisting, is there? You have simply taken what was previously an external impulse (your anger, impatience, perfectionism, etc.) and brought it inside. Feel the strength of it, the force of it. If you find it difficult to accept and deal with, can you imagine how others might feel when confronted by it?

Do not fight your resistance by pushing it under the surface; neither should you give in to it and react as usual. Observe it by making a note of what you are experiencing at that moment. Usually, it is enough to mentally repeat the word *resistance* to yourself. Sometimes, we simply need to jolt ourselves into realizing that the situation that is causing us so much distress is temporary, not a matter of life and death. At the precise moment while you and another driver are worried over who will seize a parking spot, someone else is facing real suffering like starvation or poverty. Road rage and other forms of violence are symptomatic of how quickly we externalize our problems. The answer may be that we need to have more kindness for ourselves so we can pass it along to others.

Experience: *Noble Silence*

Some years ago, I was invited to a New Year's Eve celebration given by a good friend. Although I wanted to attend, I distinctly remember not feeling in a talkative mood that night. But instead of avoiding the party, I made a conscious decision to say very little. If others wanted to interact with me, they would just have to carry the load.

While I did not have the slightest idea how this would play out, I was surprised at the results. My initial discomfort changed into contentment and, eventually, enjoyment as others seemed only too happy and willing to open up. Several people whom I had never met before expressed a desire to meet with me again. Driving home that night I reflected on what a good time I had had, despite saying very little.

Visit a monastery and you will find that silence is not a

problem. I know of a Buddhist monastery that posts the sign "Noble Silence" on the dining room wall. Noble silence means setting an intention to remain silent. Words are used only when necessary. This does not mean there is no communication. On the contrary, not using words forces us to look around more, to pick up the cues of others without having to say the words. Most often, lunch was quiet in the monastery. If a monk's bowl was empty, another monk would pick up a bowl of rice or food and offer it without saying anything. I also find that silence promotes mindfulness and more care in actions.

For this experience, begin by trying to be silent for an hour in the morning. If this is not possible, then try to speak only when spoken to. Do not sing in the shower. Do not talk to your spouse, cat, dog, or yourself. Ideally, it is useful to let those in your household know of your intention—so they will not be offended. (They may be offended anyway, which will give you more reason to practice patience and forbearance!)

If you inadvertently say something, do not get upset. Just start your silence once again. As a by-product of being silent, you may hear your mind chattering more than usual. Just take a deep breath and let it go. Silence is not just abstention from speech. Think of it as noble silence—a way to experience awareness without the static of speech getting in the way. You may want to keep a journal of your experience with being silent.

As you become more comfortable with silence, you might want to extend your period of silence into hours, or even a day. There are silent retreats that last from several days to weeks at a time. That may seem like an unbelievable length of time. But of course, it is all relative, since many of those who train to become Tibetan lamas undergo three-year silent retreats!

Another good way to experience noble silence is during mealtime. Try to eat your breakfast or lunch in intentional silence. While eating, for example, you could reflect with each bite on giving patience and forbearance to others.

Let your noble silence help you to listen and see better. Use your time of noble silence to ask for guidance. Use it to hear the Divine and seek what is deep within. The agricultural genius George Washington Carver, for example, used a period of silence each morning to listen to the secrets of plants and flowers. Extend your noble silence to others, so that their voices may be heard. Noble silence is not competitive or argumentative. Instead, it is open, expansive, tolerant, and without limits.

Principle 4: *Ethics*

He set my feet on a rock
and gave me a firm place to stand.
He put a new song in my mouth.

—Bible, Psalms 40:2–3

One story in spiritual lore tells of a man who visits a monastery looking to discover if a monk's life is really any different from that of people living in the city. The man carefully studies the monks throughout an entire day. He watches as they sit in meditation. He watches as they eat lunch. He watches as they talk with one another. He even watches as they clear the dinner table and wash the dishes. At the end of the day he takes all his notes and writes up a report, which he proudly shows to the abbot. The abbot smiles as he reads the report, his grin growing larger with each sentence. Finally, the man can take it no longer.

"Tell me, abbot, what do you think of my report?"

"You have described our actions in great detail, my dear sir."

"Then I am right in reporting that you monks do all the identical things that a person outside of the monastery does?"

"Not exactly. You see, you left out one very important point," answers the abbot.

"And what's that?" blusters the man.

"That when we eat, we eat. When we walk, we walk. When we sit, we sit. When we talk, we talk. And when we wash the dishes, we only wash the dishes, nothing more."

The man is speechless, his face beet red, as he realizes the great difference between living with and without deep awareness and mindfulness.

ECHOES OF MORAL VIRTUES

The ancient principle of ethics, or *sila paramita*, expands our experience of both moral virtues and mindfulness. It is this principle that helps us answer questions like, How do I live a moral life? How can I make skillful choices that nourish my life today and plant the seeds for future growth? Why should virtues matter when so few seem to care about them? While these are tough questions, they are also necessary ones. Mastering and living with virtues free us from the tangle of suffering. They give us a more direct route toward living a good life by liberating us from potential emotional poisons.

When most of us think of moral virtues, we tend to imagine them as written in stone—rigid and intractable. Reflect for a moment on a particular "truth" in which you believe very strongly. Is there any space for another viewpoint, or do you believe that your way is unquestionably right? Suppose, for example, that you believe in total honesty at all times. Per-

haps you are brutally honest with your feelings about someone else's actions, attire, or behavior. Yet this "honesty" is based
on *your* perceptions, *your* judgments, *your* beliefs, is it not? Is
it possible that under certain circumstances a rigid belief can
do as much harm as good? When discussing ethical guidelines, keep in mind that your awareness of how you use them
can make all the difference.

Throughout the world's wisdom traditions, similar moral
virtues get reprised in different ways. Consider the Bible's Ten
Commandments—ironically, written in stone. Let us look at
what five of those commandments tell us:

> You shall not commit murder.
> You shall not commit adultery.
> You shall not steal.
> You shall not give false testimony against your neighbor.
> You shall not covet ... anything that belongs to your neighbor.

Each of these can be seen as a contract for social order in
the external world. They set down the gold standard for behavior with relation to others. These same codes are found in
other wisdom traditions as well. They are almost identical to
raja yoga's five *yamas*, or restraints:

> nonviolence
> nonstealing
> truthfulness
> nongreed
> chastity and faithfulness

And, they closely echo the five Buddhist precepts for the
laity that ask us to:

1. refrain from intentionally taking the life of any living being;
2. refrain from taking what is not given;
3. refrain from lying or speaking what is false;
4. refrain from committing any sexual misconduct;
5. refrain from taking any substances or intoxicants that affect
   mindfulness.

There are many ways to interpret and use these similar sets of moral guidelines. For example, they can be viewed as external, behavior-based laws. In addition, they can be seen as the basis for personal purification and spiritual transformation. It is this dual nature that makes the ancient principle of ethics so essential.

Restrictions on behavior would not be needed if we did not already act out of violence, greed, sexual misconduct, lying, and mindlessness. Part of experiencing this ancient principle is to feel the regret, acceptance, and acknowledgment of our behavior—whatever it might be. This means we do not have to judge our actions on an absolute scale that turns us into either a saint or a sinner. Instead, we can simply view our actions as part of a continuum, or a circular scale.

On this circular scale, there is no such thing as ultimate and perfect honesty, ultimate and perfect nonviolence, and so on. As mentioned earlier, there is no unmixed good and bad. Each point on the scale is connected to all the others in a nonending loop, so there are no real opposites. We may not always know that what we do is entirely beneficial. Nonetheless, we *can* aspire to ask the nitty-gritty question used by spiritual teacher Ram Dass: Does it serve?

THE ALCHEMIST'S POWER

You have the power to transform yourself and your life. Yet that power will remain dormant unless you first regret the damaging actions and behaviors of your past. Regret is something that many of us refuse to accept into our consciousness. How many times have you heard someone declare, like a badge of honor, "I wouldn't change a thing," no matter how many people were hurt. Truly, some of us would rather live in denial than accept what we see as a stain on our character or ego. Regret does not mean we need to live in the past with guilt. What it does mean is that we can acknowledge our missteps and resolve to take better ones in the present. Notice I did not say "in the future." The time to make different choices is *right now!* Socrates echoes this principle with his own succinct interpretation: "Don't be embarrassed to become better at the end of your life than you were to begin with."

Regret is a necessary ingredient for change. Regret represents an awareness and desire to become more skillful in the future. That is how it acts as a catalyst. Instead of judging and blaming ourselves for having been wrong, we can simply accept that we were unskillful. *We need to couple a heightened awareness and mindfulness with skillpower in order to make spiritual progress.* Only then can we have the alchemist's power: the power of a vow to change, the power to purify the spirit.

Within this context, the commandments, yamas, and precepts are actually proactive staples for building spiritual strength and living the right kind of life. While they are formulated as "restrictions," they also represent a skillful and wise approach to living. Let us look at the precepts in greater detail. For the "glass half full" crowd, to adhere to the precepts means vowing to be more awake and skillful. It gives us each moment to:

1. embrace loving-kindness toward all beings,
2. embrace generosity,
3. embrace truthfulness and honesty,
4. embrace joy and contentment,
5. embrace mindfulness.

Most importantly, the precepts are restorative cures for the illnesses and wounds of the mind—such as denial and guilt—that can impede our ability to be mindful of the moment. Each precept gives us a clear standard toward a life that is not harmful or selfish. Here are guidelines that say to us, "Do not delude yourself, do not lie to yourself about your unwholesome actions. This is the right way."

The great Buddhist sage Padmasambhava, for example, often said that we should not disregard even the slightest thought, action, or deed:

If you want to genuinely practice the Dharma,
do what is virtuous,
even the most minute deed.
Renounce what is evil,
even the tiniest deed.
The largest ocean is made from drops of water.[1]

Then there is the practical side. Regardless of your personal faith perspective, do not the precepts reduce suffering and make life easier? They ensure that each thought and act produces the right kind of *karma*—a universal law of cause and effect that ripples through the universe. Some believe that these ripples follow us, affecting us not only in this lifetime, but the next. However, you need not believe in the concept of reincarnation or sin to recognize that the values you choose to live by at this very moment deeply affect you and others.

If I steal from or harm another, for example, I may alienate my friends and family, or even get caught and spend time in prison. For years to follow I may hinder my desire to find employment, vote in elections, and so on. Then, too, there is the inner anguish that I may experience as a result of my harmful actions. Self-blame, remorse, and sorrow represent another kind of karmic effect. On the contrary, if I give generously, I will probably not be remorseful nor put in prison for an act of generosity or kindness!

Repeat the precepts (yamas, commandments) on a daily basis to bring your life and habits into greater focus and coherence with your heart. We are taught that little white lies are OK. But where do we draw the line? Likewise, where do we draw the line with sexual misconduct? Even the news media make it appear that those who cheat—such as on a spouse or partner—are somehow honorable so long as their partners know or approve. We need to know when we are discarding self-discipline on behalf of pleasure. True honesty begins at home.

In the foreword to Mahatma Gandhi's *Vows and Observances*, his grandson Arun writes of how he learned the importance of adhering to the *right* vow at a very young age. His experience also shows why the taking of precepts is the first step on a very personal journey:

> One day during my early teen years, I got into a playful argument with my sister, Sita. For six months, she said, she would eat just one meal a day. I made light of the vow.
>
> "That is easy. Anybody can do that." Sita caught the bait and retorted, "Well, why don't you take a vow and show us what you can do?"
>
> "Sure," I boasted. "I can live for a whole week on

bananas and milk." It was an idle boast. I had no intention of carrying it out. Our parents, who were watching
the repartee, were curious to see where it would end, and
the moment I made my remark Mother decided to teach
me a lesson.

"I take it that is your vow?" she said. "You will now
have to undertake it." I was trapped.

In the Hindu tradition of our family, a vow is sacred.
Once you utter it, you have to go through with it. There
was no escape. So the following week I lived on nothing
but bananas and milk, and for several months thereafter,
I couldn't stand the sight of bananas and milk.

The taking of vows is a part of Hindu practice, but it is
also a universal form of personal discipline. It prepares
one for adversity. So one takes a vow to give up something that is very precious. It also teaches one to value
one's word, because once you have taken a vow, there is
no one watching to see whether you observe it diligently
or not except your own conscience.[2]

Take a vow to follow the precepts with greater awareness and you will change your life—today and in the future.
No, they do not guarantee that you will become a "perfect"
person. But they will point you in the right direction and help
you wear your own kind of protective armor against making
harmful choices. A life lived with guidelines such as the precepts is a consciously aware and awake life. Personally, I feel
that if you were to get nothing else from this book but a commitment to the precepts, then you would be well on the path
to living kindness.

Experience: *Awaken to the Precepts*

Why do we often act with violence? What causes us to lie, steal, and cheat? The wise teacher Krishnamurti often said that we cannot truly be nonviolent until we understand the roots of violence that exist within each of us. What is the nature of violence in your being? Violence is not only physical. For example, can you detect even its subtle effects—such as trying to impose your beliefs or will on others? Is your lack of impatience or shortness with others a kind of violence? It may be useful here to think about the positive attribute of nonharm to others, which is loving-kindness. Where your loving-kindness is stilted you may reveal undetected harm and violence.

Detecting and becoming aware of our nonviolence is the first step. Next, we need to find the roots of violence, as Krishnamurti, the Buddha, and others suggest. Emotions such as anger, fear, hurt, jealousy, envy, and other negative feelings can all result in violent lashing out at others. If you have a repetitive behavior that hurts others, now is a good time to dissect it under the microscope of your awareness and observation.

One point about this experience: Do not try to *force* yourself to be nonviolent. Even physics illustrates that every action has an equal reaction. The struggle to overcome a habit may only push the impulse elsewhere. That is why dieting rarely works—pushing a desire underground does not diminish it, and in fact repression or denial may make it stronger! We cannot simply force a negative desire to go away. The secret to embracing nonviolence, or any other precept, is not to push away the violence. Instead, we need to observe our violence and become fully aware of it, as well as its roots.

To begin this experience, find a comfortable chair or sit in the lotus meditation position with your back straight. Take in a deep breath and let it out with a loud *AHHHhhh*! Let go of any expectations you might have for this experience. This is not a one-time solution to healing negativity or eliminating harmful impulses. The ancient principle of ethics requires much time and effort. Whatever you accomplish at this precious moment is to your benefit!

Concentrate your mind on one of the five commandments, yamas, or precepts. Reflect on one particular virtue—such as loving-kindness, generosity, truthfulness, faithfulness, or mindfulness. Why is it relevant to you? Spend some time thinking about the effects of the choices you make. Which choices impede the happiness of others? Which enhance the well-being of others?

Now, turn your mind toward how you struggle with your own violence, greed, lying, sexual desire, and willfulness. Observe your thoughts, without judgment. If you do judge, just observe the judging. What desires are connected with each? For example, needing or forcing others to agree with you may stem from a desire for love and acceptance, or a fear of losing control. Or greed may come from a deeper fear of loss. Remember, a desire can be what you want, as well as what you are trying to avoid or escape. See if you can follow the desire or craving that underlies a habit or negative behavior.

MINDFULNESS AND THE MYTH OF MULTITASKING

When I was first told the following story by a monk, I thought it was just monastery humor. Actually, it is an oft-used moral tale about the perils of losing mindfulness. Though

I have heard more than one variation of it, the story basically goes like this.

A very dedicated monk was out collecting alms for his lunch when he wandered into the desolate country-side. He approached the only house within miles and was greeted by a woman who offered to fill his bowl with food. Glad to get out of the scorching sun he entered the house. To the monk's great surprise and dismay, the woman locked the door behind him!

"I won't let you leave here until you either kill my goat for dinner, drink a bottle of wine, or make love to me." The monk was appalled at the demands.

"I absolutely refuse," he answered, "for I have taken three vows—the vow not to harm any living being, the vow not to take any intoxicant that can lessen mindful-ness, and the vow to refrain from sexual misconduct."

The woman was unmoved by his plea. "You must choose one or remain here indefinitely." The thought of staying the night in this woman's home unnerved the monk. Hastily, he concluded that the least amount of harm would come from drinking a bottle of wine. Surely the abbot would forgive this single trespass. After all, he'd be doing no harm to anyone other than himself.

"If I drink the bottle of wine, do you promise to let me leave here with no other demands?" he asked.

"Yes, absolutely. You'll be free to go," she answered, handing him the bottle.

The wine so intoxicated the poor monk that shortly after finishing the bottle, he slaughtered the goat *and* made love to the woman.

Talk about a cautionary tale. It is easy to understand why mindfulness is one of the cornerstones of ethics. No matter how well grounded we may be in the moral virtues, we still need mindfulness to constantly guard the doors of the mind, senses, and body. Mindfulness brings us into the present moment—with clarity and awareness of each movement and choice. Mindfulness allows us to bring love into the world in a caring, compassionate, and wise manner. It awakens us to the marvel of each plant, animal, and creature that co-inhabits our environment.

Conversely, a lack of mindfulness does not just change our own lives, it also impacts those around us. Every day the newspaper heralds some tragic lack of mindfulness. Drinking and driving is one sad example of loss of mindfulness. So is falling asleep at the wheel—even cutting down the old-growth trees and forests that support entire ecosystems.

I frequently teach mindfulness during workshops. There was one occasion when a woman, Lynn, seemed nervous and fidgety after we had spent several minutes practicing walking meditation. When I asked what her experience was like, she said that the slow pace of the walking was boring because she was so accustomed to "multitasking." Mindfulness, which demands placing concentration on one place, on one thing, at one time, was just too much for her! Actually, this example shows how difficult mindfulness can be in today's world. While popular culture tells us that dividing our attention among many things is good, the reality is that we may be losing a very important skill—that of being present with those around us, and with ourselves—for an extended period of time.

Mindfulness is often elusive, like the air. Its essence seems to be about many things: being in the moment, doing one thing at a time, being aware of our bodies and senses, and having a clear intention when we do anything. Yes, it is all these things. Still, mindfulness cannot easily be grasped except through its practice.

On the other hand, have we not all experienced a lack of mindfulness at some point or another? Venerable U Silananda, one of my teachers and author of a book on mindfulness, shared some interesting thoughts on the topic with me. We laughed at one true story in particular. It seems that U Silananda once gave an interview to a reporter who wanted to explore the subject of mindfulness. After an hour or so the interview was over. The reporter thanked U Silananda and left. Moments later, the doorbell rang. U Silananda opened the door, only to find the reporter standing there. "Can I use your phone?" said the reporter, abashed. "I locked my keys in the car."

I am sure we have all done the equivalent of locking our keys in the car—if not worse. Consider the challenge of making dinner while the TV blares, the kids run through the house, the dog barks for scraps, and the phone rings. Is it any wonder we break dinnerware, misplace ingredients, or end up with a meal we do not even remember cooking? We have let our attention get too divided and distracted with the myth that we are only multitasking.

As a result, we miss out on the most important time available to us: the *now*. And, we may let ourselves be run about by every ringing bell, interruption, or electronic device that beckons to us. I am not saying we should avoid everyday conveniences, but they should not be leading us around by the nose.

BUILDING MINDFULNESS

There are some basic ways to build up your mindfulness muscles. One useful method is to first become more aware of your body and your breath. What is your body's posture at this very moment? If you are sitting, are you tense? Are your shoulders stooped or upright? Are your feet flat on the floor? Mindfulness of your body is something you can cultivate throughout the day. When you are sitting, for example, you can just note this body posture. The same goes for when you are standing, prone, or walking. Each time you make a change in your body, become aware of it.

As you begin this practice, begin to notice how many times you shift your position. If you sit in a chair, why do you change your position so often? Probably the underlying cause is discomfort—you move to find a more comfortable position. Even minor changes in posture can be precipitated by an almost imperceptible feeling of pain, cold, or numbness. (Often, for example, I rub my fingers together when my hands get cold.) The more you experience your body through mindfulness, the more amazed you may be to find out that your movements are often conditioned by some external stimulus.

You can also experience mindfulness by following your breath. Is your breath a long one or a short one? Pay attention to it. Mindfulness of the breath is no different from meditation on the breath. Did you ever watch a breath begin? Can you feel the middle of your breath? What about the end? There is also the space between breaths. You can observe it all as part of your body.

There is another important step to mindfulness, which is called setting an intention. This intention, followed by an action, is what brings mind and body together into the same dynamic moment. The mind commands, and the body commits to an action. The more deeply intention and action get connected, the closer you are to being in command of the present moment. Here is how I described making a "mindful salad" in my book *Art of the Inner Meal: The Power of Mindful Practices to Heal Our Food Cravings*:

> Mindfulness begins with intention. Your mindful salad may begin by your stating an intention such as "My intention is to chop lettuce for the salad." This single intention, however, contains many smaller intentions. These could be stated as "I intend to wash the lettuce. I intend to place the lettuce on the cutting board. I intend to lower the knife and cut the lettuce." Each of these intentions precedes an action. If you think that all this slows down the process of chopping lettuce, you're absolutely right! After more practice, though, your intentions will flow, as will the actions that follow them.[3]

By now, I hope you can grasp how mindfulness and moral virtue work in concert. There will always come a time when your determination to do the right thing will be tested. Mindfulness not only anchors you in your virtue, but supports those around you, too. As the Buddha said in the *Dhammapada*,

> When a wise man [or woman] established well in virtue,
> Develops consciousness and understanding . . .
> . . . he succeeds in disentangling this tangle.[4]

Experience: *Mindful Walking*

When I was in the monastery, I always enjoyed a twenty-minute mindful walk to start my day. Even now, I mindfully walk to the street to get the newspaper each morning. You can practice mindful walking anywhere. And you can take the methods presented here and extend them to other aspects of your life.

Wear a comfortable pair of shoes if you are going to practice walking meditation outdoors. If you want to practice inside, you can either wear shoes and/or socks, or go barefoot, whichever helps you feel most balanced. Once you are ready, make an effort to remove all possible distractions and create an island of peace and serenity. That includes not answering the phone, as well as turning off the radio, television, and computer. Finally, map out a route that you can walk in a continuous loop, without having to stop—even if it is the circumference of your room. Now, you are ready to begin. Your walking meditation will consist of four phases, each one more detailed than the last. Try to spend at least five to ten minutes during your first experiences.

Phase One. Mentally, state your intention to "take a step with my right leg." As you do so, take the actual step. As that step ends, state your next intention to "take a step with my left leg." Take each step slowly and deliberately. Keep your full focus on the step, feeling the entire movement of each. Do this for several steps. Your mindfulness should never become automatic or feel forced. Let your intention and your step become one as you spend about two minutes practicing this.

Phase Two. Now, you are going to add another intention to each step. Mentally, state your intention to "lift my right foot and move it forward." Follow through with this action and shift to your next intention to "lift my left foot and move it forward." Now, you will closely observe the lifting motion and the forward motion of your foot and leg. Feel the slow lifting and the careful movement forward. Practice this for two or three minutes.

Phase Three. Next, you will state your intention to "raise my right foot, move it forward, and set it down." As you take this action, observe the entire range of lifting, the moving forward, and the setting down of your foot. Feel the lightness upon lifting, what it is like to move your leg forward, and the feeling of your foot coming to rest on the floor. Now, state your next intention to "raise my left foot, move it forward, and set it down." Again, observe each movement and action in detail. If your mind thinks of other things or is distracted by a sound, just come back to observing and moving and setting intention. Practice this for another two or three minutes.

Phase Four. In this final phase, you will state the intention to "raise my right foot, move it forward, set it down, and shift the weight from my other leg to this foot." Repeat the intention to take a step with the left foot, adding the intention to "shift my weight to the left foot." As before, experience for a couple of minutes what it is like to set the intention, move, and observe your movement.

After you are comfortable with using all four intentions, you can continue to practice with all four whenever you walk mindfully. Experiment and see how closely you can observe your movement while maintaining your balance. Some who practice walking meditation move extremely slowly. Others walk at close to normal walking speed. I find that something in between feels more natural for me. Eventually, you will find a pace that feels right for you.

Mindfulness can be extended to other kinds of experiences, such as mindful eating. To experience eating in this way,

you can set intentions for picking up the food with your uten-
sil, bending your arm, opening your mouth, and chewing. As
you set the intention to chew, you can feel what happens to
the food as it changes from solid to liquid in your mouth. You
can observe the changing flavor, as well as all your desires
relating to food—including your likes and dislikes. There is
not any thought or action that is outside the realm of mindfulness. Take it all in, and make each moment as clear, awake,
and luminous as possible.

Principle 5: *Simplicity and Meditation*

People want you to be happy.
Don't keep serving them your pain!
If you could untie your wings
and free your soul of jealousy,
you and everyone around you
would fly up like doves.

—Jelaluddin Rumi,
Birdsong: Fifty-Three Short Poems

It is morning. Bright sunlight streams through the open window in my office as I meditate. Sounds from the outside filter in, too, easily distracting my anxious and unsettled mind. Thoughts of all the tasks I need to do later in the day keep popping up. At some point my mind shuttles them away to a less demanding place. Why not, I think, do these tasks another time—maybe tomorrow? I return to my concentration and breathing when what sounds like a voice not my own comments in a mocking, yet gentle tone, "Not today?" I am stunned.

It is as if a brilliant light has been shined into the dark recesses of my consciousness, illuminating for me a subtle pattern of procrastination of which I am not fully aware. It is a pattern that complicates my life, causing worry and anxiety. Instead, I am offered an alternate strategy that is simple, direct, and straightforward: Do today what needs tending today.

Now, whenever thoughts of putting things off enter my mind, I cannot help but remember, with a smile, the question "Not today?" After all, this is living kindness toward myself.

FINDING CLARITY

The ancient principle of simplicity and meditation blends together two complementary ideas, the paramitas of *nekkhamma* and *dhyana*. Interestingly, the earliest school of Buddhism uses the term *nekkhamma*, while the later ones use the term *dhyana*. Actually, these are inseparable, and the outcome of experiencing both is similar, much like diving into two ends of the same pool. *Nekkhamma* is sometimes translated as "renunciation," although its core meaning is about retiring into spiritual life and finding liberation from the attachments and worldly entanglements. Then there is meditation, or *dhyana paramita*, which represents the means for learning to let go of entanglement and engaging life's spiritual center. Thus, the principle of simplicity and meditation promises a more simple and spiritually meaningful life. It is a life that lets us find blessings in the little things.

But where and how do we begin to craft a more simplified life? What would such a life look like? What changes would this kind of living kindness require? Ralph Waldo

Emerson gives us this clue: "If we live truly, we shall see truly. . . . When a man lives with God, his voice shall be as sweet as the murmur of the brook and the rustle of the corn."[1]

The Buddha, in the *Dhammapada*, expands on the vision of simple, true living with the following wisdom:

The true master lives in truth,
In goodness and restraint,
Nonviolence, moderation and purity.

Fine words or fine features
Cannot make a master
Out of a jealous and greedy man.

Only when envy and selfishness
Are rooted out of him
May he grow in beauty.

A man may shave his head
But if he still neglects his work,
If he clings to desire and attachment,
How can he follow the way?

The true seeker
Subdues all waywardness.
He has submitted his nature to quietness.[2]

For the Buddha, living simply is achieved when our inner and outer worlds are in harmony, without constant tension. Like a mirror, each clearly reflects the other. Think for a moment about the Buddha's "quietness." This does not mean being silent. Anyone can be silent and still experience inner turmoil. This quietness is born of clarity. It is clarity that comes

when the chatter of fervent desires, attachments, and unhealthy emotions is extinguished. This laserlike clarity helps
cut through or transcend any mess—that of relationship, finances, or otherwise—with which life presents us. Only then
are we free to "follow the way"—a way of peace and aware
choices that brings our external life into congruence and harmony with our inner feelings.

Suppose that you gain greater clarity about the roots of
your own violence and selfishness. You might, for example,
choose to alter certain aspects of your life that affect the environment or other beings. However, living simply does not
mean you have to pack up all your belongings and sell them
on E-bay or give them to Goodwill! When you think about it,
material objects are only one aspect of what it means to live
simply. There is an entire dimension of spiritual experience
that is at the heart of simplicity. From this perspective, it matters less how much "stuff" you have in your life than how
able you are to step toward peace, clarity, meditation, and spiritual development. If removing some clutter helps, then fine.
If not, that is OK, too.

Still, it is valuable to ask, What does a simple life actually look like? How can I simplify my life in real ways that
promote and support my need for inner peace?

THE AMISH AND LAS VEGAS

Much of this chapter involves meditation. But simplicity
is not just about sitting down quietly for a period of time,
breathing, watching your mind, and being alone. While meditation is crucial to developing self-knowledge and clarity, it is
not meant to be a solitary path. There is also the meditation
and reflection that you apply to daily choices that determine

your lifestyle. Meditation does not stop when exiting the meditation room. It continues.

The challenge of living simply is to be more open-minded and more available to others, and to bring living kindness into your living choices. You do not have to stop observing and being mindful just because you are having a conversation, preparing dinner, or going shopping. It is vital to craft a lifestyle that supports spiritual pursuits and values, and vice versa.

Let us take a moment to consider two vastly different communities—the Amish and Las Vegas. I was introduced to the yin/yang contrast between these communities while attending a class—"Amish/Las Vegas: Polarities in American Lifestyles"—taught by Greg Crosby, a compassionate teacher and psychotherapist. As he explains it, "The Amish and Las Vegas are symbols of two polarities within ourselves and our society. Las Vegas represents instant gratification, materialism, risk, impulse, excitement, and individualism. The Amish symbolize simplicity, plainness, selflessness, community, slow change, and humility."[3] Exploring these dynamics, or polarities, can help us become more aware of their presence in our lives.

In Las Vegas, the individual's needs, desires, and pleasures take center stage. Las Vegas is all about glitter, spectacle, consumption, and personal satisfaction. What matters most is catering to the individual, not building a community. Crosby also makes the point that the prosperity of Las Vegas has caused other communities to see it as a successful model for their cities. Bear in mind that beneath the surface, present-day Las Vegas also represents the interests of major corporate owners and their shareholders.

In contrast, the Amish community stresses the importance of work over instant gratification, friendship over status, and the community over the individual. In part, the Amish have maintained their core values because they have been slow to adopt every technological change that comes along, however convenient it may seem at the time. However, rather than reject all technology, they sometimes make compromises.

These compromises may appear odd, such as allowing riding tractors, but only if the rubber wheels are removed. Also, the Amish use telephones, but not in the house. A phone booth is positioned outdoors, where it is shared by many families. While there are some appliances in homes, these operate by using alternate power sources because electricity is not permitted in the home. And although the Amish may ride in cars during emergencies, or even rent them from time to time, they are only allowed to own horse-drawn buggies for day-to-day transportation.

While some of these choices may appear inconsistent, they have one thing in common: they have the effect of slowing things down, and thus simplifying, life in some ways that are not at first obvious. No electricity means no television or video games. Most teenagers, for instance, join an Amish youth group, where they spend time playing noncompetitive games, singing, and eating together. In addition, the Amish are also a community with many rituals. Rather than have an established church building, services rotate from household to household. Having their own schools and farms for sustenance gives them a strong sense of belonging, independence, and identity. While as young adults the Amish are given a period of time to explore the outside world—the metaphorical Las Vegas, if you will—very few choose to leave the community.

What can we learn from the Amish lifestyle? First we can take home the concept of slowing down. For example, do you impulsively answer the phone every time it rings, even though you are involved in a personal conversation or having a meal?

Do you drive down the street when you could just as easily walk? Is your day planner crammed with so many appointments that you lose track or are always stressed about your lack of time? If these questions describe your lifestyle, know that you are not alone. Our culture seems to pride itself on speed.

However, even if you maintain a hectic lifestyle, you can still find opportunities to slow down or moderate the pace. Some suggestions include setting aside a part of each day when you can be alone, whether to take a rest, read something that makes you smile, reflect upon the day, or just meditate. Walk whenever possible, which is beneficial to good health and also lets you experience your surroundings more deeply. Each step taken in mindfulness can be a step taken in gratitude for your entire body and state of well-being.

Also, consider making a special meal once a week. This might mean preparing dinner from scratch, inviting over a friend, or beautifying the table setting with the addition of candles and flowers. If you have not taken a day off in a long time, you may want to slow down in areas of your work or social life. Slowing down enhances each mindful moment. You may awaken to just how few possessions are required to bring joy and pleasure into your life.

In chapter 7 we will explore the principle of truthfulness, which offers a method for living in simplicity, without entanglement. One kind of truthfulness is "nonstealing," which means that we do not take anything that is not offered. Taken a step further, we can expand nonstealing to encompass nonpossession. Nonpossession does not require giving everything away and living in poverty. But as in the Amish example, it implies that we can do without those possessions that are not truly needed or that hinder our spiritual pursuits.

The idea of plainness is another Amish concept that can

be adapted to modern life. Basically, plainness renders comparison with others—in terms of material things—practically meaningless. Everyone's buggy is pretty much identical. Similar clothing, hair styles, and lack of jewelry create an equalizing effect. Plainness removes those distractions that magnify the "I," "me," and "mine" and separate us from others. I am not saying everyone should look like everyone else. There is no harm in having preferences, such as liking a favorite color, a designer product, or a gourmet food. The difficulty arises when our personal "Las Vegas" dynamic is out of balance with the "Amish" dynamic and overshadows all else. Besides, what really makes you, or anyone, special is the enduring quality of living kindness, not your hairstyle or clothing. At least, I hope not.

Here are a few suggestions for how even a little plainness can simplify living. Instead of worrying about a product's brand name, pay more attention to its function and usefulness. You may also want to examine the consequences of letting a particular technology into your life. Technology comes with a price, and sometimes that price can be less time to spend with those who matter. Yet we invite new products into our lives each day—from cell phones and DVD players to additional cable channels—giving little consideration to the long-term results.

One participant in the Amish/Las Vegas class had recently received a DVD player as a gift. He voiced several concerns about this new technology to our group: What would he do with his extensive collection of videotapes? He would need to buy a new, larger TV that was compatible with the DVD player. Buying a new TV would require purchase of a larger cabinet to accommodate the TV and DVD player. Lastly, he wondered how much more time would he spend at home as a result? To his credit, he was giving the issue a lot of thought and had not yet opened the DVD box!

True, introducing a new technology is not a monumental change. But even small, incremental changes can alter the focus of our lives over time. And so, you may want to begin by asking yourself questions such as these: To what extent has my life become dependent on technology? What does it mean to live a simpler life? How much entertainment and stimulation do I really need? Do I get enjoyment out of the simple things in life, like a sunrise, a flower blossom, a meal? Am I considered "high maintenance" by my partner or friends? What desires nag at me constantly? And if those desires and urges were suddenly gone, what would my life be like? What would it feel like to know I have everything I need right now? And if I had that, would I be happier, more free? Sometimes, being plain or slowing down just means living with moderation and knowing what matters most

A DAY TO REST

Another way to experience simplicity is to take an entire day of rest. Not a "day off," but a day of focused spiritual renewal—such as the Sabbath day found in the Bible. For one day, liberate yourself from the encumbrances that you think you cannot do without. See if you can go without using your car—or without using any mechanical devices at all.

Take a stroll instead of driving to your favorite restaurant. Read instead of watching television. Spend time communing with nature or a neighbor; lessen the pace and enjoy the sense of connectedness that it offers. Wait a moment longer before speaking. Listen to others, and listen to yourself. Strive to find the beauty that exists in the world and in nature. Inhale deeply the miracle of each fresh breath of air. The great American naturalist John Muir knew well the restorative power of the natural world: "Everyone needs beauty as well as bread, places to play in and pray in where Nature may heal and cheer and give strength to body and soul alike."

Finding simplicity and peace, either through nature or meditation, lets us see the entire world in a new light. Several years ago, for example, a homeless lady used to frequent a corner just up the block from where I once lived. My initial feelings toward her, I must admit, were less than generous. There was a time when I would have likely dismissed her outright. Fortunately, my meditation practice provided me the opportunity to slow down and listen to my attitudes and judgments on a daily, moment-to-moment basis. Most importantly, it gave me the freedom not to be bound by them.

I decided to approach the woman. After inquiring about her plight, I learned that Margie (not her real name) once lived in the neighborhood. She had been married and had two grown children. A family-related tragedy had led to her subsequent mental and physical problems. Although her children and neighbors had arranged for an apartment, she had rejected their offer. Because of Margie's harsh living conditions I chose to help her. From time to time, on my way to the grocery store, I would ask if she needed anything. Her requests sometimes seemed odd, but I always did as she asked while I said a silent blessing for her and others in need of help.

Living kindness does not complicate life. It opens us up and (en)lightens the heaviness and suffering that we may find around us. Welcome this open, simple compassion into your office, your home, and your relationships. Your life will be more fulfilled in return. Meditation has paved the way to softening my heart and letting me realize that others, especially those in need, are not too much different from the rest of us. In the long run, I think it has helped me be more receptive to the plights of others. For that I am grateful.

Much like the Amish practice of slowing down life, meditation slowed down my thought process, dissolving its complexity and letting me see the simple truth. Meditation can act as a mirror for the simple Amish lifestyle. Each practice, internal and external, of clearing away the clutter supports the other.

BENEFITS OF MEDITATION

The wonder of meditation is that it shows how to let go without trying too hard. In this sense it resembles sports, where we have to be at our best, alert and in the zone, but totally relaxed and calm at the same time. Meditation has the effect of simplifying mental clutter. Little by little it removes those obstacles that block clarity and cause confusion.

Through meditation we learn to apply skillful, focused attention, which helps us to recognize the bare truth about reality and ourselves. Meditation trains us to be awake and present in the now, which is really the only place to fully experience the other guiding principles. With it, we can experience living kindness without the ego, judgments, desires, and labels that have been added, layer by layer, onto reality. The Buddha declares in the *Dhammapada* that there is nothing so sweet and joyful as being awake:

> He is awake.
> The victory is his.
> He has conquered the world.
>
> How can he lose the way
> Who is beyond the way?

His eye is open,
His foot is free.
Who can follow after him?

The world cannot reclaim him
Or lead him astray,
Nor can the poisoned net of desire hold him.

He is awake!
The gods watch over him.

He is awake
And finds joy in the stillness of meditation
And in the sweetness of surrender.[4]

While the practice of meditation is shared by the major
wisdom traditions, various techniques and expressions of it
can seem quite different. For Hindus, meditation is one of the
spiritual disciplines of yoga—anchored in the idea of abstention—that leads to liberation and knowledge of the divine
Self. There are many variations of Hindu meditation, from
using breath to repeating *mantras*, or sacred words. Christians
can engage in contemplative prayer as a way to be in direct
communion with God. Muslims often avail themselves of
zikr, which is the remembrance and invocation of God into
one's presence. For many Jews, prayer is sometimes indis-
tinguishable from their meditation, which is often related
to the word *kavanah*, which aims for directed sacred consciousness. Kavanah meditation is usually associated with
prayer and includes such practices as repetition of sacred
words, mental images, and verbal questioning. In addition,
Judaism possesses more than one ancient form of contemplative meditation. Likewise, the various schools of Buddhism

teach and encourage many types of meditative practices.

Later in this chapter you will experience a traditional Buddhist meditation that uses the breath and the mind—with some intriguing variations—as well as contemplative meditation that is more intuitive. Even if you have done meditation before, I find it is always useful to get steeped in it time and again. You never know what new subtleties may be revealed. Do not be fooled into thinking that meditation is simply about the breath. It offers an experience that constantly opens the door to living kindness.

During Buddha's lifetime, meditation was synonymous with the idea of mental development or training by which enlightenment was attained. Given the benefits and nature of meditation, it is easy to grasp how meditation trains the mind to be more still, focused, and creative. Regardless of the method used, you will likely experience some benefits as you grow increasingly more familiar with meditation practices.

One basic benefit of meditation is the power to steady the mind. After all, it is impossible to meditate if your attention and concentration are weak and muddled. By meditating, you will increase the strength of your mind to do almost any activity. That means you will be able to learn better, read longer, and stick with almost anything that demands your continuous mental faculties. It also means you will be better able to focus your mind on breaking habits or loosening the grip of harmful choices and patterns. In fact, you can intentionally use meditation for healing or other specialized purposes.

Meditation also has the power to generate one-pointedness, or absorption, that transforms the mind. Essentially, this means the mind is quieted, still, and reflective, while at the same time relinquishing all negativity. You will no longer need to cling to repetitive thoughts and attachments, nor to the negative desires in which they may be rooted. This is a natural by-product of steadying the mind and concentrating on an object—such as on your breath or the rising and falling of your diaphragm—during meditation. As you experience this absorption, you may feel an unusual sense of well-being, calmness, and inner peace.

This benefit holds the potential for retraining and transforming your mind's thought patterns. You will transform anger into love and compassion, greed into generosity, and impatience into tolerance. This is a gentle benefit that slowly but surely moves you toward a better, happier, and more wholesome life.

One of meditation's more unusual benefits is its infinite organizing power. This means that meditative practice can generate synchronicities and a greater awareness of all the ancient principles. *Synchronicity* is the term that the pioneering psychologist Carl Jung coined to describe "meaningful coincidences." These meaningful events reveal the existence of a continuous web of wholeness that binds and coordinates all things, without regard to time and distance. Physicists have observed this phenomenon by examining quanta—one of the basic packages of energy in the universe—and finding that they exhibit the property of nonlocality, which means that particles appear to communicate over a distance. This mimics exactly how synchronicity, long-distance healing, and other paranormal effects seem to take place. In *Unfolding Meaning,* physicist David Bohm says that beyond the illusion of separateness is "an interconnecting network of quanta weaving the whole universe into one."[5]

A series of synchronicities, for example, happened shortly before the release of one of my books. I could hardly go anywhere—from a seminar about the twelfth-century mystic Hildegard von Bingen to a monastery retreat—without sitting next to the religion reporter or features editor at a major newspaper from a city where I would be visiting on my book tour. I soon overcame my own limiting belief that these fortunate meetings were merely accidental.

Then, one evening while on the way to a friend's party, a most unlikely place to meet anyone related to the book, skepticism gave way to clarity. Climbing out of the car I said to my wife with an air of certainty, "I know someone tonight is going to want to do something with the book. I wonder who it will be?" Sure enough, I met the radio host of a popular Los Angeles culture show. Before leaving the party he invited me to appear on his program, which was to be aired on Thanksgiving Day.

The interview was very memorable and moving for me because when I was asked if I had any final words, I said a Thanksgiving blessing for the people of Los Angeles. This gave me the idea that I could say blessings for the audience on all my radio appearances, even if it was not a holiday. So I worked it in whenever I could.

There is not anything supernatural about synchronicity. Like gravity or magnetism, it is a result of an interconnected reality that is unobservable by our senses, but that generates the physical world and its laws. Still, we have to awaken to the possibility of synchronicity before we may even be able to recognize it.

One more benefit of meditation is how it raises and broadens the conscious view. Through constant, dedicated practice, you can gain transcendent knowledge and bliss. This is a state of conscious awareness that transcends the dual nature of normal reality and the normal thinking mind. That dual nature says that you recognize yourself as an individual and others as separate from you. There is an "in here" and an "out there." In a transcendent meditative state, however, the observer and the observed become one.

As you explore the ancient principle of meditation more deeply, do not get caught up in trying to "achieve" any of the above benefits as a goal. It is enough to know that they may appear and to simply continue with your meditation. Do not hang on to them, do not cling to them. If you do, then you will miss the point of meditation and simplicity altogether. Again, from the *Dhammapada*, the Buddha describes both the challenges and the benefits of meditation:

A wise man should pay attention to his mind,
Which is very difficult to perceive.
It is extremely subtle and wanders wherever it pleases.
The mind, well-guarded and controlled,
Will bring him happiness.[6]

SACRED SPACE

Many people find it useful to set aside a sacred space for their meditations. This can be an entire room, the corner of a room, or even a space normally used for something else. If you decide to hallow the space, do so in a way that reflects your personal and unique sense of the sacred. Consider reciting a blessing over the space to consecrate it. Or add a picture of someone whose spiritual life and values you admire, such as the Dalai Lama, Gandhi, Martin Luther King, Father Thomas Merton, Jesus, Mother Teresa, Teresa of Avila, or Buddha. You could do as one friend of mine did and commit to memory a special short poem or verse like this one by Saint Francis of Assisi before starting your daily practice:

Lord, make me an instrument of Your peace.
Where there is hatred, let me sow love;
Where there is injury, let me sow pardon;
Where there is doubt, let me sow faith;
Where there is despair, let me sow hope;
Where there is sadness, let me sow joy.
O Divine Master, grant that I may not so much
Seek to be consoled, as to console;
To be understood, as to understand;
To be loved, as to love.
For it is in giving that we receive,
It is in pardoning that we are pardoned,
And it is in dying that we are born to eternal life.

You can also add a sense of ritual to your meditation by lighting incense or a candle. But when all is said and done, your surroundings are not the practice. Your sacred space should enhance and hold your practice, not be a distraction. A monk I know who spent some time in a Burmese jungle monastery likes to say that he still carries the forest with him in his heart, wherever he goes. So even if you are not in your sacred space, you can do the same.

Exercise: *Creating and Ending a Breath*

Once your space is set, sit on a chair or with your legs crossed on a cushion that is placed on the floor. Keep your back straight, but relaxed. Place one palm in the other, with your thumbs touching. Take a long, deep breath. Did you feel your diaphragm rising as air filled your lungs? Did you notice, too, how your attention was focused on the physical body during that breath? At one level, meditation is as simple as breathing in and out, watching your breath rising and falling. With each inbreath the abdomen rises, and with each outbreath it falls. Or you can focus your attention on your nostrils, observing each breath—in and out. There are many different styles of meditation, but this is the fundamental starting point. You just follow the breath.

A story from the Buddhist canon tells about a monk named Sona who could not maintain the right level of effort and concentration while meditating. Either he grew tired and fell asleep, or his attention became so intense that every little thing distracted him, thus making focused concentration impossible. The Buddha himself came to Sona's aid, using the example of how the tension on the strings of a harp needed to be adjusted in order to make music. If the strings were too tight, he said, the harp would produce no sweet sounds of harmony. If the strings were too loose, no sound would come out at all. The Buddha then explained, "Similarly, Sona, if energy is applied too strongly it will tend to restlessness, and if energy is too lax it will lead to lassitude. Therefore, Sona, keep your energy in balance and balance the Spiritual Faculties and in this way focus your attention."[7] The Buddha realized, from his own experience, the need for moderation and a "middle way." So, too, do we need to find moderation and balance as we tune our own instruments of body, mind, and spirit.

You can follow a middle way by not breathing too hard or stiffening your body too much. Though it may take some practice, try to keep your breath regular. Do not strain or breathe too deeply. It may take more than one meditation session until you find a comfortable breath and sitting position.

At some point, your mind may wander. You might be thinking about a past event or memory, something that is happening right now—like a fly buzzing in your ear—or about some future business meeting that you are worried about.

When you notice that your mind has wandered, gently bring it back to the breath. No matter how many times the mind scoots off, simply bring it back. Even if you think, Oops, there goes my mind again! just bring it back and continue breathing. Do not get upset. This just tells you that you have temporarily lost your focus and that your concentration needs more work.

The mind is capable of creating many thoughts each second—thousands, according to the Buddha. Yet many who are new to meditation are shocked when they first sit down and hear the uncontrolled clatter, clamor, and chaos of their thoughts! Some believe, mistakenly, that their minds and thoughts have suddenly accelerated into hyperdrive. That is not so. What is more likely is that they have never really listened to themselves this intently before. The physical sensation of the diaphragm rising and falling, or air passing by the nostrils, should help keep you focused. But if the breath near your nostrils is too subtle for you to feel the air coming in and out, try taking a little stronger breath.

Another good way to steady the mind on breathing is to set an intention for each breath. Before each inhalation think, "Intent to create a breath." Then, as you exhale think, "Intent to end a breath." Or you could say, "Creating a breath" and "Ending a breath." This practice of setting an intention will do more than just place your attention on your breath. It will bring your mind and body into sync. Each thought will be followed by an action, over and over again. Eventually, when you are more centered and concentrated, you can drop the intention and just focus on the breath itself.

What is a good time to meditate? That depends on your personal situation and how alert you are at different times of the day. A morning meditation break will prepare you for the day. A short meditation during your coffee break at work will charge your creative batteries. Some people prefer meditating in the morning, when they feel attentive and wakeful. However, if you are fully alert, meditating in the evening will do you no harm. In fact, it may help you release the day's tensions and problems, thus setting the stage for a restful sleep. If you find yourself falling asleep, then meditate earlier. The only time that is not really advisable for meditating is immediately after a meal.

Wherever and whenever you decide to meditate, take a vow to spend at least ten to fifteen minutes a day practicing your breathing meditation. Commit to doing this for at least a month. After that, try to increase the length of time to twenty or thirty minutes daily. If you follow this method, you should feel more relaxed, tranquil, energized, creative, and alert. Since meditation is portable, free, and takes up no space, why not carry it with you wherever you go?

CONTEMPLATIVE MEDITATION

Every tradition has some form of deep contemplation that lets us encounter the Divine or garner a more knowing sense of our relationship with this mysterious and wondrous universe. Contemplative meditation does not focus primarily on the breath, although breathing is used to quiet the mind. Rather, it guides us to embrace questions and reflections that can lead to greater self-understanding and empathy with all living things. It may, for example, cast light on a personal puzzle. Or it may leave us experiencing any number of emotions. Whatever happens in contemplation is open, undetermined. All that is required is a genuine intention to be present for whatever happens. This intention is not a petition for anything, but is a direct and genuine effort to make ourselves available to the Divine, which is *already present and approachable*.

Intention in contemplation, as in mindfulness practice, is a critical step. You first need an intention to find your divine connection. What is more, you need to embrace with deep faith that you will indeed do so! Father Thomas Keating, a modern-day teacher of Christian centering prayer and contemplation, writes in *Open Mind, Open Heart* that contemplative meditation is not about relaxation, but rather "a method of moving our developing relationship with God to the level of pure faith."[8] He believes that even if we do not feel a deep faith, we need to set an intention to rest in the presence of the Divine.

When you think about it, this makes sense. Can you imagine, for example, sitting down at the dinner table without the intention to eat? Your experience will not be the same as if you were hungry and really wanted to savor a delectable meal. The same is true of contemplation. A banquet of knowing is available through the ancient principle so long as you ready yourself.

In Christian contemplative practice, a sacred word—such as *Jesus, love, Father*, or *peace*—is used as a focal point to set the mind on its goal. Keep in mind, though, that the purpose is not to maintain strict attention on the chosen word, but to surrender oneself to deeper knowledge and the Divine. Sacred words are employed in other traditions as well. The Qur'an, for example, offers the ninety-nine different names, or aspects, of Allah. The Hindu tradition has hymns for the "thousand divine names of the Lord," as well as for the Divine Mother. The Bible alludes to many names for the Divine. Then there is the well-known phrase that evolved over the centuries. Known as the "Jesus Prayer," users repeat over and over a variation of "Lord Jesus Christ, have mercy upon me, a sinner." Many persons use the Jesus Prayer without saying "a sinner." Others shorten it to "Lord Jesus Christ, have mercy."

There is no one right way to choose a sacred word. As a matter of fact, you need not be confined to a divine name. The idea here is to use a word that means something to you, something that will help you to go deeper into experiencing your relationship with all around you. I once spent a few days at a Benedictine monastery to learn and practice contemplative prayer. From the start, I was pleased to discover that the object of my focus could be whatever word or phrase was meaningful to me, from more commonly used words like *shalom* or *Lord*, to more specific religious phrases like the Hindu *sat-chit-ananda*, which translates as "being-consciousness-bliss." At first I experimented with the phrase "Thou are that" without much success. So I changed midstream and tried another—until I found one that made a stronger connection for me. Afterward we shared our experiences. The range of emotions and feelings was truly impressive. A couple of people felt bored, while one felt frustrated. Others found that contemplation let them rest in a deep, divine presence.

This is important to bear in mind when beginning to contemplate. Do not let your expectations set you up for a fall. This is an intuitive, faith-oriented—even devotional—practice. Your experience will not be the same each time. The promise of contemplation is that it brings us into the realm of the uncertain, the unknown. That is sublime, is it not? To be present, with no expectations, demands, or judgments. Contemplation lets us feel deeply exactly because it places no boundaries on our experience.

Why begin with a sacred word? It is really a doorway through which the presence of the Divine, or self-knowing, can enter. Of course, this does not have to be a word at all. You could ask a question, like the one Hindu sage Ramana

Maharshi used as his lifelong mantra: "Who am I?" Or you could do the type of meditation described by author Aryeh Kaplan in his book *Jewish Meditation*, which is to

> be focused on anything—a stone, a leaf, a flower, or an idea. One allows the subject to fill the mind and then uses it as a means to understand the self. It is a type of mirror in which one can see oneself in the light of true Reality. Using this mirror, one can see the Divine within oneself. . . . When one looks into this mirror and sees the Divine within oneself, one can also communicate with the Divine.[9]

Exercise: *Sacred Word*

As you sit with your intention, trust that your sacred word, object, or other reflection will help you go beyond rational thought. You need not repeat the word continually, but rest beside it and inside of it. Feel how this beacon can reflect into your heart-mind the divine presence or greater self-knowledge. This is where you nourish your living kindness with wisdom, effort, and patience. All the ancient principles will help you in your seeking. If your mind drifts, patiently and gently bring it back to your stated intention and your sacred word. If you need to say the word again, you can do so, but mostly, stay open to receiving what is already yours!

Take the time to sit in a silent place as you practice contemplative meditation. Devote from twenty to thirty minutes of sacred time to let yourself feel whatever comes—from grace and compassion to forgiveness and even negative emotions like hatred, anger, boredom, and frustration. Do not deny what you experience. Do not feel compelled to explain it, either.

For, as the wise mythologist Joseph Campbell once said, "God is simply our own notion of something that is symbolic of transcendence and mystery. The mystery is what's important."

INSIGHT MEDITATION

Meditation can do more than help you to pause, relax, and release. Insight meditation is an ancient Buddhist practice that engages your mind at a deep level to explore the true nature of self and ego. If you really think about it, we have no choice but to use the mind to interpret the world around us. Even all of mankind's "objective" scientific experiments are first devised by the mind and then observed by the mind. When Einstein's theory of relativity showed how reality depended on the *observer's* relative view of things, the very foundation and idea of an absolute, objective reality were forever shaken. The current study of quantum physics offers tantalizing evidence of an even more subjective reality—one where our very consciousness and observation alter the results of the experiment. So despite Descartes's view of "I think, therefore I am," he really had it backward!

Actually, as Thomas Merton and others have pointed out, it is our awareness that leads to "I am." Reality, then, begins with a pure form of awareness. It is an awareness that exists without the added weight of our self-identity and all the other layers we add onto things. Can you imagine what it would be like to jettison all this extra weight?

Before our mind colors any event with perceptions and feelings, there is bare awareness. This is our basic awareness, stripped of any kind of labeling. So, an apple is not red, juicy, and good. It just *is*. Did you ever wake up to a noise or open your eyes and notice an object before you were fully awake?

Or were you ever so awed and overwhelmed by a beautiful sunset that you were at a loss for words? That is bare awareness: experiencing without anything extra.

There are many ways we place additional layers on top of basic awareness. While some sensations that we experience are physical ones, the feelings associated with them are mental. If you step on a nail, for example, part of the sensation is physical. Your toe or foot tells you that you have stepped on something sharp. However, the experience of the feeling of pain takes place in the mind. Or suppose you are feeling hurt or angry. Again, the experience of pain is in the mind.

Even our perceptions, which are how we filter our sense feelings, are in the mind. Let us go back to that nail you might have stepped on. If you are getting married and you step on the nail while walking down the aisle, you might be embarrassed and consider it the worst thing that ever happened in your entire life. But if you stepped on it while working on your job at a construction site, you might feel angry that you were not more careful. When we hold an ice cube in our hands, when we taste an apple, when we hear a loved one's voice, we form perceptions and opinions for each—as being pleasurable, painful, good, bad, and so on. Our perceptions, judgments, and opinions, then, happen in the mind.

Even our volition, or will, which impels us to do something or avoid something—as in my earlier example of procrastination—comes from the mind. In the larger sense, volition can be viewed as being a state of mind. Just like there is "peace of mind," is there not also "greed of mind," "anger of mind," "envy of mind," and "avoidance of mind"?

These ways of experiencing the world through the mind—sense feelings, states of mind, perceptions, and volition—were what Buddha called aggregates. These four, together with the physical characteristic of form—which is part of any living or inanimate object—make up the "five aggregates" that Buddha used to describe the characteristics of our conditioned world.

Are these characteristics bad? Of course not. They just *are*. It is how we observe, interpret, and crave them that shapes our reality. The good news here is that because most of our experiences ultimately end up in the mind, each of us can use our bare awareness to closely observe them and learn from them. Even more encouraging is that it is what we choose to do with them that counts. That is where meditation comes in. It liberates us, ever so slowly, from being slavishly attached to those things in life (aggregates) that cause suffering for others and ourselves. Just like the breath rises and falls, comes and goes, so does our experience of the aggregates. Yes, some experiences may be more persistent than others, but eventually they all fall away.

What does this mean? Suppose your feelings were hurt by something you believe someone did to you. In meditation you can also watch those feelings arise and fall without any attachment to them. You might note that feeling mentally by saying "hurt, hurt," "emotion, emotion," or "memory, memory." You would use the same naming procedure whether your feeling is that of lust, fear, envy, greed, hunger, or other kind of desire. By giving it a name, you are identifying it, and you are also recognizing that it is impermanent. As long as you can let it go—even for a split second—you are also releasing your attachment to it.

You can also name external sense objects, like the sound of a car horn or a ringing telephone that jolts you out of your meditation. You could mentally name the sound by saying "noise, noise" to yourself. Then, if the noise continues, you may get annoyed or irritated, at which time you could either note your emotional state of mind as "emotional" or simply "judgmental." You might even ask yourself this question: Are these noises and thoughts jumping into my mind, or is my mind going out and grabbing them?

This shift in perspective puts you in the driver's seat, does it not? Instead of being a helpless recipient or victim of what is happening around you, you are in charge. *You* shape your reality, not external events or others. You decide whether to hold on or let go. That is why it is necessary to observe the desires, emotions, ideas, and things to which you cling.

By clinging, you also resist changing. You become stuck in place and, as a result, are less free to choose. Clinging makes you a slave to your desire or thought. You *must* have that object of your desire—that sweater, that girlfriend, that computer, that house, that high SAT score—or you just cannot be happy! I am not saying that you should not set goals, even wild and outrageous ones. But there is a thin line between being the master of your goals and having your goals be master over you. You can still be excited and have passion for what you are doing without being so attached to the outcome. If you are feeling stuck, worried, depressed, or stressed out, then you may need to look at those things to which you are clinging—including your expectations and goals. They may be doing you more harm than good.

This analytic form of meditation shines a light on the true nature of all things—including your "self"—as part of a constantly changing and impermanent world. One question that you can add in to your meditation experience from time to time is, "Who am I?" Let that question guide you to contemplate an answer. Who is doing the listening, the meditating, and the speaking? See if you can locate the point where your inner voice comes from. Is the concept of "you" as one solid entity really true? Even your ego, your beliefs, your identity, your personhood changes daily. So, are the labels that you place on "George," "Susan," and yourself really accurate? What rising and falling aggregates comprise a human being? By contrast, try to imagine a pure, natural consciousness that is fluid, expansive, and unlimited.

In the end, do we not need to release each moment as it comes and goes? If we hold on to any moment we will only be hanging onto the past. If we anticipate the next, then we are living in the future. Only by releasing living kindness into each new moment can we be here now. It is a great place to be.

Experience: *Meditation on Sensation*

The following intense breathing meditation practice can be used by anyone, but it is especially useful for those meditators who feel extreme pain in their joints, back, and other body areas while meditating on the floor in the crossed-leg position. During this meditation, you will be able to very closely watch the sensation of any acute pain you may be feeling.

Because this meditation is strenuous and requires a great degree of energy and effort, it is not for everyone. Try this for only five or ten minutes at most to start. See if it helps you overcome either pain or lack of energy and drowsiness. First, get settled in your meditation position. In this exercise, it is necessary for you to cup the palms of your hands together, one on top of the other.

For this meditation, you will take strong, rapid breaths. If at any time you feel light-headed or think you are hyperventilating, then slow down your breathing immediately. I have practiced this meditation for up to an hour at a time without experiencing any light-headedness. Also, do not be surprised if you feel your body temperature rise during rapid breathing.

Each inbreath will be completed in the length of time it takes to count "one-one-thousand." Then, you exhale rapidly, in even less time. However, you will not be using any mental thoughts to pace or count your breaths. Once you get the inbreath and outbreath rhythm, just keep breathing rapidly, without pausing between the breaths. Even though the inbreath and outbreath are not of equal duration, try to find a balance between them. Your head and body should be still.

With the deep breaths you are taking, you will definitely feel the movement of air past your upper lip and nostrils. That is where you want to focus your attention. Feel the sensation of touch with every single breath. But do not follow the air into your body; just put your energy into drawing the breath as deeply as possible, which will make your concentration that much more intense. Even though you may grow tired, try to maintain the pace. If you do have to slow down a little bit, do so. Still, continue to take a good, firm breath that is stronger than normal.

Now, here is how this meditation helps deal with pain. Although you may feel pain in many places, pick that one place where you feel the most intense pain—say, your left knee. Now, take an inbreath and hold it. At the same time, you can clench one of your cupped hands in the other. As you do this, place your attention right on the pain. (Do not note "pain, pain" as in insight meditation.) While you are holding your breath, observe the pain until it goes away or becomes less severe. Then relax your hands and begin breathing rapidly again.

Each time the pain becomes acute, hold your breath, clench your hands, and focus on the pain until it dissipates. If you hold your attention on the pain, you will find that its intensity comes and goes. And sometimes, the pain just disappears altogether!

Where does it go? It is not that pain is not real, but the nature of it is much different than you think. Use this meditation to help you compare the mental anguish that you sometimes feel and the sensation of pain that you suffer. You may not want to use this meditation all the time, but to build energy and explore the nature of sensation and pain, it is very useful to have in your spiritual toolbox.

Principle 6: *Wisdom*

Life is like a ten-speed bike. Most of us have gears we never use.

—Charles M. Schulz,
from *Crazy Wisdom*

As a boy growing up in Chicago, I took frequent family camping trips to southern Illinois, Wisconsin, and Michigan. To me, one of the most amazing wonders of the Midwest was the Mississippi River. Its distance from bank to bank was far greater than that of other, more ordinary rivers I had seen. The force of its current seemed far more swift and potent. And its colorful history, from the legendary travels of the French "voyageurs" to Mark Twain's writings, transformed the Mississippi into a mythic figure—not just to me, but for the American spirit. That is why I will never forget a cruise that I took down China's Yangtze River as an adult. I could only gaze in awe at the Yangtze's stunning magnificence and immensity, which seemed to dwarf that of the great Mississippi.

My own experience reminds me of a tale described by the fourth-century Taoist sage Chuang Tzu in *The Book of Chuang Tzu*. One autumn, so the story goes, the banks of the great Yellow River bulged to such an extent that "it was impossible to distinguish an ox from a horse" from one bank to the other. This made the Lord of the Yellow River very happy— it was confirmation that his river was undisputedly the grandest of all. He flowed downstream with the raging waters until they arrived at the North Ocean. When the Lord of the Yellow River peered at the vast body of water he was taken aback. Unlike his river, this ocean had no visible end or boundaries whatsoever. Then, the ocean enlightened the river with these words:

> A frog in a well cannot discuss the ocean, because he is limited by the size of his well. A summer insect cannot discuss ice, because it knows only its own season. A narrow-minded scholar cannot discuss the Tao, because he is constrained by his teachings. . . .
>
> . . . If someone has perfect Virtue, it is not possible for fire to harm, nor for water to drown, nor for either cold or heat to affect, nor birds and beasts to injure him. Not that I say that he dismisses all these things, but that he is able to discriminate between where he is safe and where he is in danger.[1]

A GARDEN OF WISDOM

The ancient principle of wisdom, or *panna paramita*, asks us to look past our own boundaries and judgments. It challenges us to break through hypocrisy and ignorance. It urges us to become more skillful in answering the needs of others.

Only then can we bring the wisdom of clear vision to our decisions.

Examples of this wisdom abound. We are fortunate to have been graced with a garden of wisdom from around the world and across the ages.

> To be wronged is nothing unless you continue to remember it. (Confucius)

> To be blind is bad, but worse it is to have eyes and not to see. (Helen Keller)

> The wind cannot shake a mountain. Neither praise nor blame moves the wise man. (Buddha)

> Don't concern yourself with the faults of others. Use the scouring powder of wisdom to keep the rooms of your own mind bright and spotless. By your example, other persons will be inspired to do their own housecleaning. (Paramahansa Yogananda)

> Truth conceived by the mature soul is expressed as wisdom. (Inayat Khan)

> Whoever wants to see the form of his naked soul should make wisdom his mirror. (Aristotle)

Have you ever visited a Zen garden? Some such gardens are designed with fifteen different stones. Wherever you position yourself in the garden, however, only fourteen stones are visible—one is always hidden from view. Likewise, wisdom does not reveal its truths without putting in the effort to look at a situation from all angles and perspectives.

We might choose to perform an action—any action—but it is wisdom that shows how to perform that action with skill. Only with wisdom, for example, can you understand how to gain wealth without doing harm—just like a hummingbird takes nectar without hurting flowers. Only with wisdom can you apply discipline to your life without becoming rigid. Only with wisdom can you distinguish between true compassion and those actions performed for misguided or selfish reasons.

Perhaps that is why wisdom is so important in our religions. In Buddhism, for example, wisdom is one of three training groups, along with ethics and concentration. And from the Judaic and Christian traditions, the Bible teaches: "Blessed is the man who finds wisdom, the man who gains understanding, for she is more profitable than silver, and yields better returns than gold. . . . By wisdom the Lord laid the earth's foundations" (Prov. 3:13–19). Similarly, the Qur'an (31:27) cites wisdom as one of the attributes of the Divine: "And even if all the trees on earth were pens, and the ocean ink, backed up by seven more oceans, the word of God would not be exhausted: for God is infinite in power and wisdom."

None of the ancient principles can be experienced fully without an accompanying wisdom. The truth of wisdom is powerful because it pierces the veil of darkness and ignorance. Wisdom cannot be taught, but it can be known and felt from a place of compassion and acceptance of truth.

THE WISDOM OF ACCEPTANCE AND COMPASSION

Much unhappiness stems from not accepting things the way they really are. "Why don't I have a better job?" "Why can't I find the man (or woman) of my dreams?" "Why is life so hard?" "Why don't others—such as my mother, father, boss, child, partner, etcetera—understand me?"

I know of a man, John, who had a string of unfulfilling relationships. This happened despite his badly wanting to find someone with whom he could settle down. I was surprised when John confided in me that his last girlfriend was a closet alcoholic. As I listened, he said something even more revealing: "I don't blame her for any of the problems we had. I know now that it was 100 percent my fault." By taking on his share of responsibility for his choices (maybe more than his share), John saw the truth of his situation, in particular his own need—at some level—to be in an abusive relationship. But it was only when he experienced the deep acceptance of forgiveness and compassion—for himself and his girlfriend—that John was free to correct his course and move forward.

How can each of us learn to live with the ups and downs that life has in store for us? One way is to accept reality as it really is—unadorned, without the chains of illusion and ignorance. The Buddha addressed this issue during his first talk, which occurred shortly after attaining enlightenment. Originally, he had planned on teaching this to only two of his former mentors. But he realized that the Dharma—the teaching, the path, the way, the truth—was meant to be available for all genuine truth seekers. So he dedicated himself to teaching and liberating from suffering all those beings with only a "little dust in their eyes." He spent the next forty-five years of his life walking across India fulfilling his promise. For those of us with only a little (or even much) dust in our eyes, what follows are the eyedrops that replace illusion with clear vision and acceptance.

How many times have you heard someone say, "All I want is to be happy," as if happiness were some static object that could be purchased at the store, later to be possessed and locked away for safekeeping. The first dose of eyedrops tells us that this permanent thing called happiness is an illusion, a master magician's trick. Rather, daily life is in some way unsatisfactory, flawed, inconsistent, unhappy, incomplete, filled with suffering, or diminished over time. It is important for us to think about whether or not this is true. One example of this is our own emotions. Do you know anyone who has been perfectly and blissfully happy his or her entire life, without end? How about for years? Well, then, what about days? Well, if not days, then how about hours? Minutes? In reality, do not our emotions drift past like clouds passing in the sky? This is not to say that we do not feel happiness and joy. But in truth, we can be happy one moment, sad or upset the next. Look closely at the things around you to determine for yourself whether or not there is suffering in the world that all beings experience.

The next dose of eyedrops illuminates the nature of change and impermanence. It explores why it is painful—and impossible—to try to hold onto permanent, static happiness or any other object of affection. Even when we are totally satisfied with something—like a new car, a new house, or a new whatever—it gets old, does it not? I do not just mean "old" in the sense that our experience of it is no longer new, but rather that the thing itself changes. A car's engine oil deteriorates with use, its tires sometimes go bald (not to mention the driver), and its exposure to the environment causes the exterior body to get chipped and lose its lustrous shine. Every physical thing undergoes some kind of a wash cycle that is part of its natural wear and tear—like it or not, we get rinsed, washed, spun, and rinsed again! Even at the subatomic level, particles collide and molecules keep shifting.

In short, there is no permanence in the conditioned, cause-and-effect universe that we inhabit. We, our loved ones, even our most cherished treasures are subject to impermanence and change. No matter how hard we try to believe in the illusion of permanence, we cannot permanently hold onto anything. This is how and why incompleteness tends to pervade our lives and our experiences. This does not mean that we will never be happy. But this eyedrop lets us accept that happiness and satisfaction are also temporary and imperfect because the conditions that allow them today will certainly change in the future.

And, even if nothing else changes, we do. Nature sees to it that all things are born, age, and die. Even our bright, mighty sun will someday be extinguished. This is reality. It might seem harsh, and we can try our best to deny it, but if we look around we find it to be true. During the Buddha's time and for many centuries afterward, it was not uncommon for monks to watch bodies decompose in graveyards or to meditate on the thirty-two body parts described in Buddhist teachings. This seems gruesome and macabre in a culture like ours where everything is sanitized and disposed of the moment it dies! The point of the practice, however, was not to serve as a gross-out. The purpose was to look very closely—with an impassive twenty-twenty vision—at the truth about death and what will happen to each of us one day.

However, it would be a big mistake to think that these eyedrops engender a pessimistic or fatalistic approach to life. If anything, the awareness that comes from these eyedrops offers hope for liberation and freedom in the moment. You may think, for example, that your individual "self" is a solid, single entity. How is it, then, that we are composed of 98 percent water? Science has shown that at the atomic level, even the most solid substances—a table, chair, or wall—are essentially empty space. Even the cells of our bodies eventually die and regenerate every seven years throughout our lifetime. So in reality, there is a whole new "you" or "me" living here every seven years. Obviously, there is a lot more (or less!) to each of us than our limited senses can detect.

Yet is it not odd that somehow we continue to cling to many of the same constricted, even hurtful, views and ideas throughout our entire lives? We may try to hold on to our youth, beauty, fame, hairline, loved ones, cherished beliefs, and so forth. Fortunately, these eyedrops break through the illusion of our limited self and limited views. They let us see the true nature of self and all things with clarity and openness, and through the prism of unlimited love.

Of course, it is convenient to pretend that suffering does not exist. We can easily chase after more and more new, novel, and exciting experiences, more and more objects to give us temporary pleasure, relief, and happiness. There is only one problem with this strategy: we can never get satiated, never get enough. We may fill ourselves up, but we never really get *fulfilled*. In the end, we will simply stumble from cheesecake to cheesecake (take that literally or figuratively).

Then, there are the eyedrops that get to the root of our blurry vision. Basically, the engine that drives our dissatisfaction is sensory craving, desire, and attachment. Remember, suffering applies to *conditioned experience*. Craving and desire are conditioned, are they not? Our senses, our memories and habits, our bodies, and our consciousness constantly react to things that cause us to have thoughts and desires. More often than not our desires cause us to become *attached* to certain things.

While walking through the grocery store, for example, I pass by the pastry section. Perhaps I am already hungry. Or perhaps the aroma of a favorite cake, its appearance, and a vivid memory of its sweet chocolate flavor and creamy texture stimulate my desire to eat. Or maybe I buy this cake each week, creating an even stronger habit of desire. Thus, my desire for the cake and my attachment to it are conditioned. Craving does not just arise from out of the blue. If we could trace back all our thoughts, even subtle ones, we would find that they have an origin, or a cause.

While desire on the one hand is about wanting something, it can also be about *not* wanting something. This is best represented by the common image of the carrot and the stick. A horse runs after the carrot because of desire, but it also runs away from the stick because of aversion. So, is not aversion really a desire in reverse? Perhaps I desire not to have something because of my distaste, dislike, or fear of it. But again, my aversion is still conditioned and dependent upon something else.

Each desire or aversion causes us to act and think in ways that result in yet even more desires and cravings. Like a dog running after its tail, cause and effect chase each other around in circles. "But," you may be asking, "don't we need to desire things?"

It is certainly true that not all desires are equal in terms of how they create suffering. Some desires, of course, are simply a matter of preference that might not really make much of a difference. Wanting to paint your house pink instead of brown will not harm anyone—except maybe the fashion police.

And yes, there definitely are many good desires. For example, without the desire for food we would not stay alive. It is when our desire becomes an unquenchable craving or obsession, or causes us to do harm to ourselves or others, that it creates suffering and unhappiness. If you have ever been hurt because you tied your happiness or well-being to a person, place, opinion, self-identity, behavior, or goal, then you have firsthand experience of desire.

If the eyedrops up to this point are about to make you cry, fear not. By grasping and accepting these truths of reality about your own being and the nature of all around you, you can be liberated from acting as if ever-changing external or internal influences determine your fate. By accepting the nature of self, suffering, and impermanence, you bring a beneficial outlook to the world. You can accept whatever happens in your life—the sad moments and the ecstatic ones—without being defeated or fearful of a fall. You will accept and better understand the deep hunger, fear of loss, and despair that often grip others.

Once free from limiting illusion, ignorance, and desires, you can experience new, more open approaches to many life situations. Can you, for example, imagine what it would be like to live without the poisons of jealously, anger, hate, and envy? To be free of all insecurity, fear, and doubt? To live in the moment, without delusion? To face change, even death, with a sense of calm and peace? This is not only possible, but also attainable by becoming more skillful through daily effort, experience, and practice.

Perhaps you have used the principle of meditation to watch your desires? Or used patience to let go of your own beliefs long enough to show empathy to others? Or maybe you were generous with your use of kind speech when you might have been curt or even cruel? With wisdom you are free to behave in ways that reduce suffering, not increase it—for yourself and others.

If you think these "eyedrops" will not let you be happy, think again. Wisdom shows that happiness is *now*, in your every aware thought, deed, and action—not in some unrealized craving. Awareness is the key that opens wisdom's vault.

GONE, GONE BEYOND, INTO CRAZY WISDOM

There is an oft-used mantra from the *Heart Sutra*, a well-known discourse on wisdom, that translates as, "Gone, gone, gone beyond, gone altogether beyond, oh enlightenment!" Wisdom can be like a boat that carries you beyond—altogether beyond—the shores of the known by using some unconventional means. This is known as "crazy wisdom," and tales of it can be found in all traditions. There are myths of the Native American trickster, tales of the Arabic great fool Nasrudin, and even historical holy fools like the rabbi Baal Shem Tov. Crazy wisdom teachings are often full of paradox, like finding that the word *alone*, when broken in half, possesses "all one."

In *The Snow Lion's Turquoise Mane*, Lama Surya Das has recorded many teaching tales from the rich Tibetan tradition. One story, that of a crazy/wise yogi, illustrates how crazy wisdom cuts through even the smugness of pomp and ceremony:

> Once Drukpa Kunley had nothing to do, so he meandered into the midst of a great monastic gathering. It was an auspicious occasion; the monks were congregated in the temple courtyard to recite the Diamond Sutra, which explains the ultimate wisdom of emptiness.
>
> Although Drukpa Kunley looked like a mere tramp, his gleeful demeanor and authentic spiritual presence set him apart. Today many seek the sublime inner peace and fulfillment that he had made his own.
>
> In the very midst of the solemn, sonorous chanting of the Mahayana wisdom scripture, Drukpa Kunley shinned up the flagpole in the center of the courtyard, in plain sight of everyone. Then he perched on top of the

pole, flapped his arms, and cawed like a crow—creating, as usual, not a little disturbance. He began to mimic the monks' recitation.

Outraged, the venerable monks in unison invoked a traditional formula to quell the disturbance. "By the power of this sutra, may that mischievous beggar come down," they intoned.

The Drukpa obligingly began a rather theatrical descent.

The monks continued their chant, "By the power of our concentration on the recitation of this sutra, may the malicious beggar come down."

Instantly, the irrepressible divine madman reascended the flagpole.

"Parrots cannot concentrate, parrots cannot comprehend," the crazy yogi cackled.[2]

Many of those who have been courageous enough to overturn the conventions of their day—such as Buddha, Jesus, Gandhi, Martin Luther King, and others—can be thought of as practicing crazy wisdom. In his book *Crazy Wisdom*, author Wes Nisker concludes that when we look beneath the surface, crazy wisdom is really about one thing: "the death of knowledge and truth, beliefs and philosophies; the death of art forms and political institutions, nations and empires; the death of gods and goddesses, even the death of planets and galaxies and universes."[3] Let us not forget the death of the ego, the death of illusion, and the death of our own hypocrisy, sarcasm, and pretense.

You do not have to look too far to find crazy wisdom. All you need is to turn things upside down a bit. First, you might want to drop all rehearsed methods of reacting. Crazy wisdom does not fit a mold. You cannot force it. Crazy wisdom is most often spontaneous, and that is part of its magic. If you really think about it, things are funnier than they seem. If you do not think so, read the works of people like Woody Allen and Albert Einstein to put things into their proper perspective!

In the overall scheme of things, is it possible that we are less significant than we think? What do we really have to lose by letting go of what we hold dear? By seeing the humor around us?

Sometimes, you can express crazy wisdom just by your acceptance of "what is" in a new way. I can remember that when I was in the monastery, my parents did not fully appreciate the new change and spiritual quest in my life. It taught me that I could try to be accepting of what I did not understand—even my parents. If nothing else, at the least I could have a good laugh at my human foibles. So go ahead and enliven living kindness with humor and crazy wisdom. I think you will be glad you did. As comedian Milton Berle so aptly put it on the occasion of his eighty-eighth birthday, "I live to laugh and I laugh to live."

Experience: *The Wisdom of Listening*

At times we must face certain hardships without running from them. Those hardships can be physical or emotional ailments, or just difficult life or relationship situations. Have you ever been in a situation where someone lamented about a problem or situation in his or her life—and then *you* tried to solve it? If someone wants guidance, that may be useful. But other times, there is no immediate remedy. Not everything can be "fixed."

There is another path, though it may not heal all wounds. We can listen with our whole being and our warm, wise heart.

A wise heart does not stand in judgment of another. Instead, it dwells within us like a healing light. It opens suffering with empathy and love, then acts without limitation, as a mother comforts her crying baby. Empathy encourages us to let go of our own worldviews and step into someone else's shoes. Empathy does not attempt to change anyone. But it does give space and love to those who may be suffering in any of numerous ways—even dying. That may be all that is required.

Spend a day practicing wise and conscious listening. Do this at work, home, or wherever you happen to be. Do not worry about being totally silent, as in the noble silence practiced earlier. You can even ask questions of the person you listen to. But since you are listening with empathy, you will try to understand what it feels like—without making any judgment—to be in the other's situation. You might want to express, "I know how difficult this must be for you" or "I know you are suffering." If you listen with a warm heart, you will say the compassionate thing.

I happen to know of a meditation teacher who asks his students to practice each breath as if it were their last one! This does more than awaken the student to life's precious, fleeting nature. It builds empathy for all beings who must one day face their own last breath. By listening with wisdom we walk on Earth with an appreciation for the suffering of other beings.

Principle 7: *Truthfulness*

Truth can never wither because it can only be found from moment to moment in every thought, in every relationship, in every word, in every gesture, in a smile, in tears.

—Krishnamurti, *The Book of Life*

A man known as MG was once pulled aside by a close friend in order to have a private talk. A short time later, while MG and his friend were engaged deeply in conversation, a third person walked up. When the new party asked if he was interrupting, the close friend said no and invited him to join in. Though MG was "taken aback," he realized that this was the polite thing to do. Deep down, though, MG felt that his close friend's politeness was really dishonest.

Has anything like that ever happened to you? If it did, would you have had the same reaction as MG—Mahatma Gandhi? Though Gandhi conceded that the incident was a trivial one, he also thought it was a telling one. Mainly, it did not fit his definition of adhering to truth.

A QUESTION OF RELATIONSHIP

Truthfulness, or *sacca paramita*, is an ancient principle that underpins all the others. Without truth, we could never have a benchmark from which to sense and experience the other ancient principles. Truth, it seems, is one of the most highly valued principles throughout history and the wisdom traditions. The Tibetans, for example, look at the world through the prism of two levels of truth, or reality—conventional truth and absolute truth. The Hindu practice of *satya*, or truthfulness, requires genuineness and honesty without distortion. The Bible's admonitions against stealing, coveting, adultery, killing, and lying are all based on truthfulness. The Qur'an (34:49), too, wisely tells us that "falsehood neither creates anything new, nor restores anything." Without truth there is no trust. Without trust there is no order, no calm, no peace.

Many religious tales warn us that anyone who disregards or disobeys truth risks punishment—even death. I doubt very few modern people take that threat seriously! At the same time, we underestimate how small deceptions can harm our spirit and relationships, eroding them little by little. This erosion exists because we have lost a deeper understanding of what truth really stands for.

I know a young man, Daniel, who applied to college and was interviewed by some alumni. After the interview, he shared with me his feeling that things had not gone smoothly. In particular, Daniel had stumbled badly over one key question: "What is more important to you: keeping a secret or telling the truth?" It is a question I am glad I was not asked as a high school senior when I interviewed for college! Still, it is a question worth considering.

Should we keep secrets at all costs? Why do some journalists risk jail rather than tell their sources? The privacy of the priest's confessional is well documented. Even psychologists maintain a level of confidentiality with their clients. Under what conditions should we break a promise? Under what conditions should we tell the truth?

Before answering any of these questions, we need to ask, what is truth? For some, if it is written in newsprint then it must be true. For others, truth is what can be objectively shown—such as science, mathematics, logic, and conditioned behavior. For others, truth is found in what they believe in—their countries, their governments, their families, their own intelligence and capabilities. For others still, truth is encountered in what they subjectively and directly feel—sensation, love, anger, hate, compassion, and even knowing of God. Which one is correct? Actually, all of these versions of truth have one thing in common: they are all about relationship. Truth is a function of the relationship we have with ourselves and our perceived world through the prism of consciousness.

In the Oscar-winning film *A Beautiful Mind*, the nerdy and brilliant mathematician John Nash is shown as having a rowdy but caring roommate during his college years. It is only later in the film that we discover that this roommate never existed. Director Ron Howard brilliantly includes the audience in Nash's schizophrenic delusions. Like Nash, we accept the roommate as a real person. And like Nash, we must grapple with the jolting fact that some of what we embraced as real was entirely imaginary, the product of our minds! This may seem an extreme example, but are any of us that much different when it comes to fashioning the "truth" of our own realities?

Consider that even science is in flux. One thousand years ago, the prevailing science taught that the surface of Earth was flat. Even little more than one hundred years ago, it was believed that flight was impossible with anything that was heavier than air. Who knows what new, revelatory truths will be part of science another hundred or thousand years from now?

Still, we are here, now. We do not need to wait for some scientific truth to reveal how to lead a better life. Science has made life more comfortable, but it cannot show us how to bring greater compassion and love and meaning into our lives (although someday it might). Truth, however, is like a high-voltage spark that illumines our spiritual path and energizes all the ancient principles. Polonius's famous advice to his son, Laertes, in *Hamlet* continues to strike a chord centuries after Shakespeare wrote it:

> This above all; to thine own self be true,
> And it must follow,
> As the night the day,
> Thou canst not then be false to any man.[1]

Very few of us would like to think that we are not good persons who are striving to do right under most circumstances. Even dictators and tyrants believe that what they are doing is right and for the best. That is why honesty and truthfulness must begin at home with self-awareness—just as generosity, patience, and all the ancient principles do. If our most basic self-relationship is filled with deceit, then an honest and true relationship with others is impossible. What is "true" for you in your life? Are you the "good father," the "good mother," the "good teacher" without question? What part of your behavior are you quick to overlook or ignore? Is someone else at fault for what goes haywire in your life—relationships, bad

work situations, failing finances? How do we manage to repeat the same negative patterns over and over, and yet
continue to be surprised by this?

This tendency to ignore our own complicity in any given
situation reminds me of the story about a new monk who joins
a very strict monastery. On one particular day, after working
hard in the fields, the new monk is so tired that he falls asleep
during the evening meditation. Without warning, he is awakened by a sharp rap to his back—administered by the stern
head monk who wields a long, thin tree branch like a whip.
The new monk sits up straight, determined to meditate. But
his exhaustion overtakes him, and within minutes he again
falls asleep. Moments later, he feels another burning crack of
the stick—this time harder than before—across his aching back.
Irate at this humiliating treatment, the new monk rises to face
the steely abbot.

"I do not understand why you treat me with such abuse.
I have done absolutely nothing to warrant this kind of treatment!" he complains.

"It is true that I have brought the stick that hits you. But
is it not also true that you have brought the body?" With a
clear comprehension of this truth, the monk then bows re-
spectfully and returns to his meditation.

Bare honesty is difficult because our self-image often
blocks the truth. Each of us has a carefully constructed self-
image, self-identity, or ego. When this identity gets frozen, it
becomes a reference point for twisting whatever happens to
fit this frozen self-image. Suppose, for example, that I pride
myself on being a faultlessly honest person, one who "tells it
like it is," regardless of whether my family and others are hurt
by my criticisms. After all, I know that I am really doing them
a favor. Have you ever known someone like this?

What is really behind a crusade to fix others and make

them conform to our way of thinking? In reality it may be many things: personal anger, a need for love and approval, insecurity. Unless we can become aware of the causes behind our actions, thoughts, and deeds, we cannot know ourselves. If this sounds like a reprise of some of the concepts from the ancient principle of meditation and simplicity, it is. We can never get enough practice and experience of truthfulness. Until we can accept the truth, we may be destined to repeat our mistakes and the suffering that goes with them.

Experience: *Seeking Honesty*

Sigmund Freud once said, "Being extremely honest with oneself is a good exercise." Yet, some of us will go to extremes to avoid the truth. It makes one wonder, how bad and how scary can the truth be? If it is true that at times we are selfish, boring, confused, foul, thoughtless, lustful, greedy, envious, and hateful, would the world come to an end? Jesus powerfully touched on this essential need for honesty in the Bible (John 8:7) by saying, "If any of you is without sin, let him be the first to throw a stone."

Jesus' words are worth remembering, considering how much misunderstanding, ignorance, and mistrust still exist. Even in America, dissension sometimes still arises when an unfamiliar religious group seeks to open a school, temple, or retreat center in an area populated by another faith. We can only hope that people and their communities will seek to resolve these differences with honest dialogue, tolerance, and understanding.

For this experience, find a comfortable, quiet place to sit. You may want to take a minute or two to center yourself by concentrating on your breath. When you are ready, begin by saying,

> May I open up and accept without judgment all the truths about myself.

Now, rest with your self at this very moment. How do you feel about your self right now? Where are you honest, and where are you dishonest? Sense where there is discomfort. You might consider actions or thoughts about which you feel badly. How are you conflicted? Resist the temptation to "fix" things and create solutions. Just watch and observe. Remember, all of nature is beautiful because of its uniqueness. Be what you are without measuring yourself against yardsticks of your own creation (or of others).

No matter what wrongs you may have done in your life, the truth purifies and leads to forgiveness. Let yourself out of the straitjacket of confining beliefs. Look at each moment anew. Truthfulness begins in the here and now. It means experiencing your real feelings, not faking them. If you are uneasy in a social situation, feel your unease. If you believe you are supposed to be happy and perfect all the time, then you will probably need to take some very strong pills, narcotics, or drugs. What is wrong with being sad? Depressed? What is wrong with feeling grief when you experience loss? At the same time, truth lets us know that this, too, will change. It also lets us experience the happy moments, ecstatic bursts, and joyous times.

As this experience comes to a close, let yourself awaken to the truth of your present emotion with a sense of gratefulness. Know that by honestly and directly resting with whatever you feel, you do not need to deny it or be overwhelmed by it.

Once you are more honest with yourself, you can share this authentic self with others. For one day, try to be honest with yourself and others. Be honest about all your opinions and judgments, too. Seek to discover the mutual truth of the relationship before you, rather than simply imposing your personal "truth" on others. Also, try to bring your compassion and wisdom to bear as you speak. Perhaps this new way of approaching truth will remove some of the frozen ways of thinking and being that keep you from touching each moment.

Do not be surprised if this kind of honesty changes your relationships with others—which interestingly brings us back to the question posed earlier, with one addition. Again, you can ask yourself, what is more important to you: keeping a secret (relationship with another), telling the truth (relationship with oneself), or seeking the truth (mutual relationship with another, as well as the Divine)? As you can see, there is no right answer. It is all a question of relationships.

LIVING IN TRUTH

Where and how can we begin to live with truth in a way that does not impose our ideas on others? The easiest and most direct way is through our actions and speech. I can vividly remember the time, many years ago, when I was visiting Madrid, Spain. Leaving a small café, I heard a man calling out, "Señor, señor!" The man ran toward me holding out my camera, which I had left behind. Being from a large American city I was touched. Yet this kind of honesty is fairly common in many countries, even very poor ones.

While we cannot change others, we can change ourselves. One way is to begin by taking a vow of truthfulness. A vow to act with honesty is also a vow to act with integrity in our in-

teractions with others. This also means living without hypocrisy or pretension. There is a sense of innocence and joy that
comes about from living like this. When a monk leaves the
monastery, for example, he does not leave his vows behind.
When we go to work each morning, we do not have to leave
our valued principles behind. We need to be consistent in honesty and integrity. There is no reason to think that one set of
values is appropriate for the workplace, another for the home,
and another for dealing with strangers.

Each day brings new temptations and challenges. This
means that on a moment-to-moment basis you can work on
your vow. A vow is never completed, never a thing of the past.
Instead, it is right there with you, helping you take the next
step forward. You can even think of a vow of truthfulness as a
personal guard protecting you against suffering and entanglement. It also lets you live a more simple and straightforward
life. You need not be conflicted by temptation or gray areas.
Rather, you will have a direct route for taking action.

My suggestion regarding a vow of truthfulness is this:
Do not take this vow unless you really intend to follow that
path, to put your heart and soul into it—even if you know it
will be difficult. Why set yourself up for failure if you are not
really ready? This would only mean you are being dishonest
with yourself from the start. I would advise that you take your
vow in front of someone else or with a spiritual advisor or
community. A vow is not a resolution to reach some future
goal. It is a present-moment commitment, full blast.

What happens if you should break a vow of honesty?
First, you can admit your untruth. You may also want to pray
using the following words:

> By the power of admitting this truth, may I be able to
> work on this problem.

Next, you can try to amend the situation by taking corrective action. You may be able to return what was lost or taken. Sometimes, however, such things as trust, love, and confidence cannot be regained. Know that there are consequences that you will likely face, then do your best to address them honestly.

In addition, you need to forgive and find compassion for yourself. There is no sense in feeling guilt for something that is past. Sometimes, though, it is difficult to muster compassion and forgiveness for one who mistreats or abuses others —especially if that abuser happens to be you. I remember one time in the monastery when I expressed my difficulty in finding compassion for parents who abused their children. Upon hearing this, my friend U Thitzana shared a karmic spiritual analysis of what happens when a criminal commits a crime against a victim. "A spiritually awakened being," he explained, "might see these two persons in the following way. The perpetrator is like someone who borrows money and has a debt that he has to pay in the future. The victim is like a person who has made repayment of his previous debt. Even though the victim suffers, he may not have to suffer from past sins. The perpetrator must pay for his crimes and suffer misdeeds in the future. That is why an enlightened being has a great feeling of compassion toward anyone who does bad things to him or others." Even if you do not believe in karma, it is true that the person who hurts another usually suffers in this lifetime as a result. Here is where you can use the ancient principle of patience and forbearance, as well as forgiveness, to assist in healing your wounds.

You can also feel regret and remorse for your action—which is another way of saying you will act differently in the next moment. Sometimes, our actions are less than skillful. Take some time to see where your action failed you. Then, devise a backup plan that will ensure greater skillfulness and wisdom the next time a similar situation comes around. In this way, you can develop skillpower, not depend on willpower, to succeed.

POWER OF TRUE SPEECH

The other way we can bring truth into our lives is by constantly applying the right kind of truthful speech. Truthful speech is about sharing what matters and expressing living kindness in words. Some of us, however, mistake a litany of personal biases, judgments, and opinions with being truthful. Here is one example of a biased conversation:

> "Hello, Mary, how are you?"
>
> "Well, Tom, my feet are killing me. My car broke down yesterday and I think my mechanic is cheating me. By the way, you gained some weight and look a little pale. Are you OK?"
>
> "Nah, I feel lousy. I'm under a lot of stress at work, and my boss is an idiot. Anyway, I have to run. Nice talking to you."
>
> "Same here. See you around."

I am sure we have all experienced someone who shared his or her disastrous day or life with us. And yes, sometimes we may feel the need to "unload" all our troubles or partake in the social side of small talk. But in the long run, this kind of communication does not benefit us. In contrast, truthful speech encourages us to be authentic and genuine. It assists us in listening and speaking in a way that is kind, gentle, compassionate, empowering, and honest. When we find those right words we do as Paramahansa Yogananda advises: "Every word you utter should be potent with soul vibration. A man's words are lifeless if he fails to impregnate them with spiritual force. . . . Man's words should represent not only truth but also his definite understanding and realization. Speech without soul force is like husks without corn."

Too often, we speak the "truth" without making distinctions about the impact that our words will have on others. How can we determine if *what* we say and *how* we say it are beneficial? Sometimes, we may not even know that we are acting contrary to our beliefs. I know of one case where a man named Jerry had the habit of laughing, smiling, or making inappropriate remarks whenever someone was in pain. When Jerry went to visit his brother Gabe, who was in the hospital, Gabe became visibly upset at his brother's lighthearted comments about people who needed to use wheelchairs—as Gabe did. Obviously, Jerry had gone out of his way to visit his brother at the hospital on numerous occasions. He cared about Gabe, but he was totally unaware that his demeanor and remarks were insensitive. Perhaps Jerry's own discomfort with illness caused him to speak and act like he did. As a result, he could not show empathy and respond in a way that would be beneficial.

Carl Rogers, the founder of patient-centered therapy, viewed this in terms of congruence and incongruence. Congruence means that my actions and experiences are in sync with my self-awareness and self-image. If I am incongruent, then I cannot be genuine and authentic in my actions. Similarly, one of the special qualities of a Buddha is knowing the distinction between true and false speech—and which should be used. In Buddhist teachings, there are six variations of speech. The first four types are best to be avoided. These are:

1. False words that are not beneficial, and are agreeable to many.

2. False words that are not beneficial, and are disagreeable to many.

3. True words that are not beneficial, and are agreeable to many and liked by many.

4. True words that are not beneficial, and are disagreeable to many and disliked by many.

The next two types of speech are the only kind of words that a Buddha—or any enlightened being—would use:

5. True words that are beneficial, and are agreeable to many and liked by many.

6. True words that are beneficial, and are disagreeable to some and disliked by some.

Now, you may counter that there are times when false words are beneficial. For example, suppose a neighbor seeks refuge in your home to hide from someone looking to do them harm. Would you unyieldingly tell the truth and say, "Yes, so-and-so is here" if that would lead to the killing or harm of that person? No, of course not. So there are exceptions, such as saving a life, for which an untruth would be beneficial. Still, we need to recognize the danger of rationalizing and speaking of falsehoods for the wrong reasons.

Is it really possible to speak truthfully? Yes, and it becomes easier the more you commit to it. It may mean that you have to censor that critical voice inside. You may first want to listen to whether you speak falsely or truthfully to yourself. If you cannot be kind to and honest with yourself, it is unlikely you will master that skill with others.

What about gossip or exaggeration? This is something you will want to let go of as well. Becoming an ordained monk, as I learned, means giving up all with which you are intimately familiar—your name, hairstyle (all hair), clothes, luxuries, conveniences, gossip, and vanity. What is left is a treasury of moderate and wholesome speech.

The key word to remember about true speech is *beneficial*. Is what you are saying beneficial to another? Suppose I am a manager and one of my workers is not taking direction properly. There are many different ways to respond. If I shout and berate someone for taking so long to learn a simple thing, my words are not beneficial. But if I take the time to show this person a better way or try to understand the reason for his or her confusion, then I am communicating beneficially.

Beneficial language is a process. Since very few of us have developed a fully awakened manner of speaking, we will need to experience and practice this daily. Should this seem difficult, if not impossible, consider that beneficial and truthful speech is not accomplished in a vacuum. It is supported by all the other ancient values. As such, you can use patience to give you time to find the right words. You can use simplicity to help you speak more directly, without sarcasm and subtext. You can use wisdom to bring compassion to your words. You can use generosity to generate praise and empowerment. You can let forbearance keep you from responding harshly. You can use effort, ethics, and discipline to keep your vow of truthfulness at the forefront of your mind.

What should you do when you speak falsely, or find that you have thoughtlessly hurt another with your words? You can apologize or ask forgiveness. Then, follow the same steps mentioned earlier for making amends when breaking a vow. If you have a habit of offending others, even though you do not mean to, practice empathy and wise listening. Put the thoughts, needs, and desires of others before your own. Make your speech less about you and more about the one with whom you are speaking. Do not be surprised if you become more in demand and have more friends calling to spend time with you. As Thich Nhat Hanh wisely advises, "Consider each word carefully before you say anything, so that your speech is "right" in both form and content. . . . You have a right to tell another everything that is in your heart with the condition that you use only loving speech. If you are not able to speak calmly, then don't speak that day." [2]

Experience: *True Feelings*

True speech as covered thus far is about how to discriminate between false and true speech. But what do we do when someone turns the table and speaks falsely to us, or hurts us by being less than beneficial? When this happens, we have a choice. We may decide to hold a grudge. We may decide to practice forbearance, forgiveness, and compassion. Or we may decide to experience true speech and let the person know that his or her words were hurtful and not beneficial.

If you have ever been verbally abused, you are not alone. There is not anyone who has never been criticized or abused at some time in his or her life. Even the Buddha was verbally abused by a man who came to meet with him. When this occurred, the Buddha explained to the man that when someone offers a gift, the recipient has the choice to either accept it or return it. Therefore, the Buddha refused to accept the abuse and told the man he was giving it back to him. By doing this, the Buddha was frank and direct. How you decide to return an unwanted gift—if indeed that is your decision—is up to you.

The purpose of this experience is to speak honestly about your feelings—especially if someone has used words that have hurt you. Remember, the purpose of true speech is not to get back at another. It is not to make the person feel guilty or shameful. It is to be beneficial, authentic, genuine, and honest. In some cases, the "perpetrator" may not want to hear your words. Just stay in the moment with the conversation. How can you get across your point, knowing that the other person may not even be aware of his or her impact on you?

My best advice is this: Be patient, kind, and compassionate. Do not expect an apology. If you are telling someone this, it is probably because you care about him or her and value the relationship. Let the person know this. And always remember, with a smile, that while someone else wielded the stick, you also brought the body.

Principle 8: *Steadfastness*

Your work is to discover your work
And then with all your heart
To give yourself to it.

—Buddha, *The Dhammapada*

There is an illuminating tale about a man who trekked through the deepest jungles of Burma to reach a monastery where many others had been known to reach enlightenment. He asked the abbot how long his enlightenment would take. The abbot replied, "You can have enlightenment in one week. But you must meditate for those seven days in total absorption, without a single distracting thought." The man joined the monastery, thinking that he would soon have his enlightenment.

Anxious to begin, he sat in his first meditation that very morning. After the first ten seconds, he thought to himself, "This isn't that hard." Then, realizing that he had experienced a distracting thought, he quieted his mind again.

Fifteen seconds later he thought, "I've certainly medi-
tated for longer than my first attempt." And so it went. Ten
years later he was still there, trying to attain his seven days of
complete meditation!

UNSHAKEABLE WILL

The ancient principle of steadfastness, or *adhitthana
paramita*, helps you apply an unshakeable will toward meeting your spiritual objectives. With steadfastness you can be
confident about fulfilling your commitments, no matter how
steep the mountain you have chosen to climb. Steadfastness
gives you the courage to take yet another step, even when
you think you can continue no further. This principle is nour-
ished deeply by all the other ancient principles. Yet it also
stands alone.

Still, it is worthwhile to ask the question, Is there a difference between being resolute and being stubborn? When
we are resolute, then we are genuinely purposeful, resolved,
determined, and persistent. What we aim for—a deeper experience and knowing of self—is not desired out of a need for
mastery or personal gain. To be resolute is to be purpose
driven, without being fixed on a narrow, inflexible, selfish
view. When our purpose is clear, it comes with a deep sense
of humility. Steadfastness is like a gentle and persistent wind
that keeps blowing. We can always feel it at our backs, encouraging us to take the next step forward.

Stubbornness, on the other hand, offers only a limited,
unyielding, and willful view. Have you ever known anyone
with "tunnel vision"? This is usually a state of unawareness
that is basically self-serving. Anytime we are focused on only
one thing, we cannot help but miss the rest of the picture. It is

this narrow focus that causes a stubborn person to ignore the concerns of others so long as his or her needs are met. Of course, this does not mean that all forms of stubbornness are bad. It takes a lot of stubbornness to set up a well-intentioned organization. Fortunately, it is possible to check stubbornness at the door and still remain steadfast.

Where does steadfastness come from? How can anyone develop unbending will and strength to stick to a course without wavering? I am always inspired by examples that abound in the natural world. A blade of grass sprouts up through the most unlikely place: a paper-thin crack in a concrete sidewalk. The arctic tern migrates thousands of miles each year. Many species of animals make annual pilgrimages—just as our early human ancestors doggedly trailed herds of animals in order to survive. Steadfastness is in our genes. Still, we need to apply a healthy dose of enthusiasm and discipline. One way to do this is to become constantly aware of the fact that *our spiritual path is wherever we are right now.*

I am reminded of the Native American vision quest. This rigorous ritual is usually undertaken over a period of days as one travels alone in the wilderness—often without food. The goal of those on such a spiritual journey is to experience a vision that connects them to deeper meaning and purpose. A woman I know, Connie, prepared for her vision quest by creating a ceremonial shield that contained some issues that she wanted to resolve. On the shield, for example, she painted the word *path*—in the hope that her own path would be revealed during the three-day vision quest.

From the island where she and a small number of other "questers" initially assembled, participants set out at dusk. Each person was instructed to trek away from others and set up his or her own camp. The sky opened up and Connie was forced to pitch her tent in a heavy thunderstorm. She was startled when another "quester" walked past and asked, "Is this the path?" before disappearing into the darkness. Connie thought the question odd until the morning—when she discovered that her tent was directly on one of the paths circling the island. Later, she had the epiphany that her path was always with her, wherever she was. She did not have to go looking for it at all! All she had to do was be unwavering in her desire for knowing it and deepening it.

Many of us believe that we require a supernatural "vision" to help fulfill our spiritual journey. We want the sizzle as much or more than the steak. The ancient principle of steadfastness, however, teaches us that we need only experience what is present in order to have a powerful vision. As my friend Connie learned, a vision can take many different forms, and we do not need to witness a mystical white light or be visited by a supernatural being to have an insightful and clarifying vision.

Experience: *Taking a Pilgrimage*

Pilgrimage is integral to many traditions. A pilgrimage to Mecca during a Muslim's lifetime is one of Islam's five pillars. Many Buddhists travel to Bodh Gaya, where the Buddha is said to have been enlightened. Jerusalem, Mount Sinai, and the Wailing Wall are other popular pilgrimage sites. I know of one woman who for several years has made a pilgrimage to Europe looking for images of the inspiring Black Madonna.

Why is pilgrimage so popular? Maybe it fulfills a deep human need to seek for the divine source and wellspring of truth. Perhaps it is a testament to—as well as a test of—unshakeable human resolve. Whatever the cause, a pilgrimage lets us directly touch and experience the ancient principle of steadfastness.

A pilgrimage does not have to take you to another geographic locale. You may undertake a pilgrimage that expands your mind, understanding, and tolerance. Personally, I view each book I write as a pilgrimage that transports me to unexplored territory and broadens my conscious view—sometimes creating new bridges to walk across. I once interviewed a Muslim scholar who explained that the word *jihad* really meant "noble quest," though it more literally translates as "effort." For this reason, several years ago he had named his son Jihad (and you thought "a boy named Sue" had problems!). This man was deeply saddened that the word *jihad* was often identified with the idea of a holy war—an oxymoron if there ever was one. Before we parted he wished me well on my personal jihad to complete my book. His kind words of encouragement have stuck with me, and I now like to think of any worthwhile pilgrimage as a noble quest.

Whether you know it or not, your life is a pilgrimage. In addition, you have been resolute and steadfast in taking this journey—even if at times you did not know you were on it! The first part of this experience is to reveal what your life pilgrimage is all about. If you used your imagination to follow your pilgrimage to its conclusion, where would you be, what would you find? Do not put any limits on what you might discover or feel. One good way to start may be to look for a theme that seems to repeat through your many experiences. Possible themes, for instance, could be learning about the importance of love, surrender, or the wise use of power.

Sit down in a quiet spot. After you have centered your body and focused on your breath to quiet your mind, begin to reflect on these questions. Do not force it. If nothing concrete appears, you can always try later. Remember, though, that your path is where you are right now. Let that be your guide.

The second part of this experience is to envision and then create a real pilgrimage or vision quest that you will undertake. This could take many forms. It could mean visiting a spiritually significant place. It could be a beneficial project you complete. It could be a service or charity that you offer. To be steadfast in accomplishing your goal, set out very specific things to be accomplished—such as volunteering at a specific organization for X number of hours. You may want to consider choosing something that brings you into contact with others and reduces suffering in some way.

Resist the temptation to quit midstream and switch to something else. Once you are decided on your pilgrimage, stick it out to the end. Let the process and the journey act as your ennobling vision quest. Be awake and aware that each step along the way is critical—even if you should find it boring and meaningless. The purpose of the pilgrimage is not simply to get from point A to point B. It is defined and shaped by what happens to you and others along the way. Finally, do not be afraid to take a chance. Will Rogers said it very well when he quipped, "Go out on a limb—that's where the fruit is."

COURAGE OF KNOWING

Steadfastness can be derailed in many ways, by many different distractions, fears, and enticements. Fortunately, courage and fearlessness can support steadfastness and keep you on track—even during those times when you feel uncertain and filled with doubt. The epic poem and gospel of Hinduism, the Bhagavad-Gita, or "Song of God," tells the gripping story of what it takes to gain spiritual freedom and knowledge. Central to the story is a battle about to be waged over a kingdom. Fighting for one side is Prince Arjuna, who chooses to have only the divine Krishna as his ally. But Krishna cannot fight and only serves as the prince's advisor and charioteer. Before the battle begins, the prince is filled with fear and despair:

> Krishna, Krishna,
> Now as I look on
> These my kinsmen
> Arrayed for battle,
> My limbs are weakened,
> My lips are parching,
> My body trembles.[1]

In addition, the thought of hurting those who are "teachers, fathers, grandfathers, uncles" overcomes the prince with sorrow—even though these same persons would surely kill him to gain their ends. While the ensuing battle is an external one, the Bhagavad-Gita is really about Arjuna's inner struggle to awaken to the knowledge of his divine being. In this sense, to win means going to war against our own egos and identities that we hold dear. Naturally, this also entails facing our deepest fears. It is little wonder that Krishna counters Arjuna's reluctance and fear in no uncertain words:

> Arjuna, is this hour of battle the time for scruples and fancies? Are they worthy of you, who seek enlightenment? Any brave man who merely hopes for fame and heaven would despise them.
> What is this weakness? It is beneath you. Is it for nothing that men call you the foe-consumer? Shake off this cowardice, Arjuna. Stand up.[2]

If someone known as the "foe-consumer" is shaking in his boots, then the rest of us do not need to feel so bad! Like Arjuna, do we not often fear what we do not know? We do not know the truth about old age and death, so we fear them. Ignorant of our true self and being, we can easily become selfish and defensive. Obviously, the struggle to gain spiritual ground is not for the faint of heart. This epic poem reveals two important things: First, that the real foe is within. Second, that courage is a necessity for gaining spiritual ground.

There are some very good reasons to cultivate courage. Courage helps us know the unknown. If we consider that everyone is absolutely destined to succeed in lighting his or her spiritual lamp, then there is really little to fear. It also helps to remember that the spiritual journey is not so much a matter of blind trust and feeling as it is a matter of knowing and experiencing. Courage helps us take the step of bringing to light what is present at each moment.

Too often, we think that faith and trust are necessary for anything that cannot be seen or proven scientifically. But must I have "blind faith" in God simply because there is no scientific fact that a divine being or creator exists? Or can I rest securely in my personal experience of *knowing*? Consider that five hundred years ago, humans felt the force of gravity just as we do today, only Newton was not yet born to quantify it. Did that mean gravity did not exist previously? Humans instinctively knew that something held them to the ground. Long before Newton, people knew that when an apple ripened it did not fall "up." Just so today, the miracle of life, the organized nature of life, and the miraculous web of consciousness provide us with the knowing we need to declare that the cosmos is no accident and we are more than what our senses can detect.

Just because the Newton or Einstein of consciousness has

not yet been born to give us a quantifying formula does not negate our knowing of Brahman, Buddha Nature, the Great Spirit, or God as defined in various wisdom traditions. Writer and philosopher Huston Smith confirms this in *Forgotten Truth* when he writes, "The mystic vision is not a feeling: it is a seeing, a knowing."[3] And as Smith and mystics throughout history have trumpeted, this special kind of knowing is not the privilege of only a few, but the spiritual heritage of all beings. This heritage is one that has given us a mind, a body, and a conscious spirit that are exquisitely intertwined, the product of millions of years of evolving beingness.

If you really want to tap into this extraordinary heritage, you will need to be steadfast in your desire and effort to experience yourself more deeply. Do not be blinded by the insecurity and limitation of your self-identity. Develop the heart of a warrior who is ready to stake claim to his or her inheritance. Be courageous and determined to seek your knowing and awakened being each moment of the day. This *knowing* part of you already exists, and the ancient principles are tools for bringing it to light. If you remain steadfast you will eventually realize that there is nothing that anyone outside of yourself can do to take this knowing away from you or to lessen it. It is your birthright. And so, what makes someone a saint? "Instead of wondering about the mystery of life," writes spiritual teacher Deepak Chopra, "a saint lives it."[4]

Experience: *Cultivating Courage*

Courage is the by-product of skillpower, not willpower. If you are gripped by fear, it is not likely that you will suddenly be able to "will" yourself to act differently. However, if you make a consistent effort to face your fears, you will more easily take on daunting spiritual and life challenges. Having courage does not mean you will never experience fear. But your skill will give you the courage and confidence to overcome fear should it arise.

Where is fear? How can we use it to cultivate courage? Fortunately, fear does not hide unobtrusively in the corner. It is usually out front if we are willing to acknowledge it. By noticing and finding your "fear points," you will be able to address this shadow that blocks you from the light of truth about yourself.

What is your greatest fear? For many of us, fear of mortality is high on the list. Western society, perhaps more than most, seems to have placed a taboo on death. It seems sad that our elderly are sent to retirement homes or hospitals to die. Fortunately, it is not always this way. My wife's Burmese grandmother, for example, died at home with extended family present. The local monks were there, too, chanting and praying for her well-being at this critical moment. Moments before the time came, she was lucid, smiling, and at peace in her shrunken, threadbare body. She passed so serenely that no one noticed until a family friend and doctor informed everyone that her pulse had stopped.

In Tibet, the transition from life to death has typically been viewed as one of the most important events of one's lifetime. I can recall hearing about dying persons proudly inviting family and community to be present for their deaths. One man had spent a long time organizing his "going away" party. His bed was situated strategically in the middle of the room. There were many refreshments available and everything was going as planned except for one embarrassing detail: try as he might, he just could not die. Eventually everyone left, leaving the man sad that he had disappointed his guests!

So, how can you let your fears come to your aid? How

can you use them to give you courage? The first step is recognition. For this part of the experience, let yourself complete the following sentences:

"I fear _____."
"I often worry about _____."
"I really dislike having to _____."

Try not to think too hard about the answers; just see what pops into your head. Is there a theme or pattern of fear or avoidance in these answers? Or maybe you just know deep down what it is that challenges you.

Once you have brought a fear to light, you need to examine it more closely. For this, close your eyes and use the meditation described earlier to focus on your breath. Once your mind is settled, reflect on this fear. Let your mind say it. Observe without judgment and see what associations come up. Where do you feel the fear? Is it centered in your stomach, your heart? Whether you can feel a location or not, you need to feel a deep sense of forgiveness and compassion for yourself and your fear. If you find it useful, imagine yourself immersed in a white healing light. You can also repeat the following words from Buddhist loving-kindness practice until you feel a sense of peace:

May all suffering ones be suffering free.
May the fear struck fearless be.
May the grieving ones shed all grief.
May all beings find relief.

Once your fears are more present, live with them. Let them awaken your being. If you fear mortality, go out of your way to help those who are dying. Volunteer at a hospice center. Have the courage to see the truth of aging and disease and death. After all, no one will escape it.

If you fear scarcity in your life, then try to find the truth about letting go. Have the courage to look at generosity and experience it more fully. Let your fear become a remembrance of what you need to do. Do not attempt to overcome your fears with force, or you will only create a resistance to them. Instead, embrace them with gentle acceptance and grace.

While in the monastery I remember my initial fear about not eating after twelve noon each day. This fear was heightened by the fact that there was an abundance of food in the meditation hall—from fresh fruit to boxes of cookies—all offerings to the Buddha. Internally, an alarmed voice seemed to demand, "I'd like that food, and I want it *now!*" Yet instead of repressing or forcing my hunger away, I simply watched it, fascinated by how the simple act of awareness removed the emotional charge it held for me. The more I reflected on—and accepted—this hungry and craving part of myself, the more I learned that it was nothing to run from (or run to). It did, however, give me greater courage to keep on looking deeper. Used in this way, I think you will find that fear can be transformed into a positive force.

Principle 9: *Equanimity*

The pure consciousness . . . does not look at things, and does not ignore them, annihilate them, negate them. It accepts them fully, in complete oneness with them. It looks "out of them," as though fulfilling the role of consciousness not for itself only but for them also.

—Thomas Merton, *Mystics and Zen Masters*

There was a man who was unexpectedly laid off from work. A neighbor who learned of this event sadly shook his head and said, "How terrible it is that you've lost your job."

"Perhaps," replied the man.

Since the man was now unemployed, he took a walk downtown. There he bumped into an old friend and successful banker. The banker offered him a job at twice the money of his previous one. When the neighbor heard the good news, he could barely contain his excitement.

"That's fantastic!" said the neighbor.

"Perhaps," answered the man.

Two days later while working at his new job, the man slipped and injured his back. When the neighbor noticed the man hobble home, he asked what had happened. After learning the news, the neighbor was sympathetic.

"Oh, that's too bad. What an unlucky break," he said.

"Perhaps," said the man.

The next day as the man stayed at home nursing his bad back, the bank was victimized by a terrifying robbery. When the neighbor read about it he called his friend on the phone.

"What a stroke of luck that you missed the robbery," declared the neighbor.

"Perhaps," answered the man again, without missing a beat. Naturally, this story could go on and on, and in some versions it does . . . perhaps! Just like the man who used his "perhaps" to accept the inevitability of change and stress, each of us can experience the guiding principle of equanimity to invite greater peace and calm.

THE STRESS REDUCER

Upekkha paramita, or the principle of equanimity, points the way toward approaching life's ups and downs with a sense of balance, magnanimity, and neutrality. With equanimity, we are not aimlessly tossed about by every storm of pain or breeze of pleasure that blows through our lives.

In modern life, stress represents an ever-growing health problem—for mind, body, and spirit. While contagious diseases such as polio, tuberculosis, measles, and others have been greatly controlled, there has been an increase in stress-related chronic illness. It has been shown that ongoing emotional upset—think of those type A persons—may contribute to heart disease, cancer, and stroke. And those are the physical by-products. Then there are all the emotional by-products that appear in the form of aggression, rage, and depression. Stress may affect our spiritual being as well by drawing our attention and energy away from those sources that can truly nurture us.

What causes stress? It is not just those major emergencies and catastrophes, like car accidents and the loss of loved ones. Often, the causes of stress are an accumulation of little things. It may be that we are running late for an appointment and are stuck in a traffic jam—with no way out but a sense of overwhelming anger and frustration. Maybe we find ourselves in the midst of a job, residence, or relationship change. Or we may be under extreme pressure to perform for school or at work. Maybe every little thing that our child/spouse/associate/friend does or says is annoying and ready to trigger an outburst. If these scenarios feel familiar, then you may need to inoculate yourself with a dose of the inner peace vaccine: equanimity.

The purpose of equanimity is to help us maintain and experience evenness in the midst of suffering and pleasure. It gives us an attitude of acceptance and nondiscrimination toward all beings. Once we grasp equanimity, we can be better at letting things take their own course—as opposed to compulsively trying to control and react to them. Of course, this seems to run counter to our cultural bias of willfully shaping the world according to our wishes. Who among us has not ever felt the desire to "make things right"—as we see it? Equanimity gives us another choice.

One ancient story about equanimity tells of a tragedy concerning an unfortunate family that was to be executed because its members had incurred the wrath of the king. They called upon their famous relative, the Buddha, to come and help them out of their predicament. The Buddha traveled to the kingdom and heard their pleas. He also realized that it was not for him to interfere. What had led to their dilemma and karmic debt was of their own doing. So he chose equanimity and let it be. The fourth-century Buddhist scholar and philosopher Buddhaghosa aptly addressed this situation when he wrote, "Beings are the owners of their deeds. Whose (if not theirs) is the choice by which they will become happy, or will get free from suffering, or will not fall away from the success they have reached?"[1]

Was the Buddha wrong, indifferent, or cold in his neutrality? Or did he recognize that his relatives' troubles had a force of their own. By taking an evenhanded course he accepted the tragedy without adding to it or being drawn into it. Does this mean, however, that we should never take a stand? Should one express equanimity even if there is unjust treatment involved?

Equanimity does not mean that we become indifferent to suffering. But it does mean that we do not need to buy into every drama and irritant that beg us to react. One look at a daily newspaper and we will likely find disturbing stories—some seem to have no other purpose than to raise the reader's blood pressure. I once asked a friend of mine who wrote for a popular magazine what editors wanted in a story. "The outrage factor," he said, indicating that the desirable stories were those that caused the greatest response, outrage, and offense.

What is your personal "outrage factor"? What causes you to lose all sight of equanimity and calm? To begin experiencing equanimity, pay attention as you read the morning newspaper or watch the evening news on TV. Make an effort to shift into equanimity whenever you get defensive about those persons and points of view with whom and with which you do not quite agree. Even if you only accept that there is always another side to things, you will be stepping gently in the direction of equanimity. When we embrace equanimity we let go of our prejudice and resentment. Doubtless, the world will continue—for good or bad—with or without our outrage.

Experience: *Transparent for a Day*

Every action has some kind of a payoff. In the short term, losing equanimity may seem to offer some solid benefits. Holding strong opinions may bolster your self-image as being someone who is decisive and knowing. You may pride yourself on your opinions. You may even feel a moral obligation to share your point of view because others need to be enlightened—as you are. You *know*, for example, that capital punishment is wrong, and you are more than willing to tell anyone who differs with you exactly why they are misguided and you are right. You may resent others for holding obviously wrong and stupid views. Or you may like the feeling of approval you get—from others or yourself—when you win an argument. Regardless of the short-term payoffs, however, you need to anticipate how your actions may result in some long-term repercussions.

Every family struggles with what it means to create harmony. Often, it is difficult to find a balance for letting all family members be heard without recrimination. Yet in the long term, whenever someone "wins," someone else "loses." Communication can be marred with hurt feelings, bombast, and pride. An unforgiving attitude of righteousness, indifference to the feelings of others, and unresolved resentment can grow. Then, too, there are the damaging physical manifestations caused by stress. Are these consequences really worth all the effort and energy?

For this experience, begin by imagining what would happen if you put your pet "issue" on hold? What would it feel like to trust in the healing quality of equanimity? If you are up to the commitment, make a vow to suspend your opinions and reactivity for part of the day or an entire day. Let all the usual irritants pass through you as if you were so light and neutral as to be transparent. Go about your business, all the time knowing that the universe does not play favorites—everyone has good and bad times. At least, by experiencing equanimity, you need not try to add or subtract from what is.

I know of a man, for example, who had difficulty meditating because his apartment was located on a busy street. Just when he would get focused there would be a noise from outside—a car horn or children playing—to break his concentration. He became angry at the children and at himself for not having a quiet place to practice. He blamed these distractions for keeping him from meditating. In truth, he needed to realize these random sounds were not jumping through the window to grab his attention. Rather, he was reaching out and grabbing those sounds.

You can also use this day of equanimity to experience speech and words in a new way. Because none of us is perfect, there is no perfect use of words. There are times when we will all say the wrong things, negotiate without knowing all the facts, jump to conclusions, interrupt others, and even try to compete by winning arguments at all costs. What you can do, though, is to become more equal and nondiscriminating in your treatment of others over time. Treat all persons, even strangers, with kindness and openness for what they think. Do not worry about measuring your words, but rather, think about how your words measure you. This, too, is equanimity. You may even want to repeat the following intention and blessing at the beginning of the day:

May all my words and actions
be equally nourishing
to those who need them.
May my neutrality
bring me closer to the light of truth.

TEN STEPS TO PEACE

We live in a world that desperately needs peace. Yet world peace often seems so elusive as to be nothing more than a dream. Instead, political expediency and military might seem to rule the day. Is such a peace really possible? Or is it a utopian dream, never to be realized?

External, worldly peace is subject to so many different existing conditions that achieving it is like trying to turn back time. Cycles of ignorance that breed hate, brutality, and gross misunderstanding continue. Perhaps the wise course is to do our best to generate love and compassion—equally and without discrimination—for those parties involved in their painful situations. Hatred cannot heal or lessen hatred. Only love can do that. Meanwhile, we can commit to a course that does not add fuel to existing fires. Along the way we can certainly experience, cultivate, and develop inner peace.

When we are at peace within, there is no need for us to be at war with the outside world. Our inner peace and equanimity can lead by example, sending ripples of peace in all directions of our lives. Following are ten simple steps that we can apply and experience daily to promote greater peace inwardly and outwardly. The Buddha offered these steps to peace to those traveling the spiritual journey. May we all take advantage of them starting *today*.

1. *Do not cling to your desires, expectations, and wishes.* By the same token, do not attach to the desires, expectations, and wishes of others.

2. *Be grateful for what is already in your life, and that way you will never be unsatisfied.* Develop a feeling and attitude of acceptance and contentment with whatever life brings you—be it cherries, apples, or lemons. This does not mean being passive, but it does mean you need to put in the necessary effort to solve life issues.

3. *Seek both external and internal peace and experience them fully.* One way to experience external peace is by retiring into privacy, away from distraction and entanglement. This could translate as privacy at home— by shutting off the phone, TV, and other distractions. Or it could mean taking a camping trip where you can be alone with nature, beauty, and simplicity. For inner peace, cultivate contemplation and meditation. As you feel what this peace is like, keep it in your heart and take it back home with you. Personally, for example, I like to keep the monastery in my heart wherever I go.

4. *Be aware of unnecessary gossip and activities that can distract and disturb you.* In other words, simplify your life to increase conscious awareness and reduce waste. For some this might mean reducing socializing, while for others it could involve curtailing dependence on the media for news and entertainment.

5. *Make the effort to achieve your spiritual goals by all means available to you.* Find support for your spiritual devel-

opment outside of yourself, through like-minded in
dividuals or groups. Read books that can inspire living kindness. Pursue personal experiences and reach
out toward others who suffer.

6. *Commit yourself to an ethical and moral life.* It helps to
   have moral disciplines that you can follow. Morality
   is the basis of living a good life and following the ancient principles.

7. *Develop inner calm, tranquility, and serenity.* If your spiritual path is not developing these qualities, then you
   may need additional, proper guidance. The key is to
   apply yourself daily to some aspect of your spiritual
   needs. In this sense, it is very much like exercising

8. *Awaken to wisdom and intellectual maturity in your life.*
   This awakening is part of a long journey. It involves
   the process of discovery and seeking for truth. Do not
   be in a hurry to gain wisdom—rather, let it come to
   you.

9. *Work to attain liberation and release from conditioning and
   suffering based on ignorance and delusion.* Here you come
   full circle with the crux of where to seek for the seeds
   of peace.

10. *Find unique means for achieving inner freedom and stick-
    ing to your spiritual path.* A mountain has different
    curves and terrain leading toward the top. Each per-
    son resonates with a spiritual path that is uniquely
    his or her own. As the Sufis say, "There are as many
    paths as there are hearts of men." This is the miracle

of being. Follow your path deeply and with convic-
tion. Be persistent, courageous, and willing to take
risks.

By following these ten steps, you can lead a life filled
with tranquility and peace. So, in the final analysis, peace *is*
attainable. How and when you find it is in your own hands
and heart. You can heed the insightful sentiments of Ralph
Waldo Emerson when he wrote, "When some external event
raises your spirits, and you think good days are preparing for
you, do not believe it. It can never be so. Nothing can bring
you peace but yourself."

LOVE WITH EQUANIMITY

Have you ever heard of the saying, "If you let a bird out
of a cage and it does not come back to you, it was never really
yours"? The guiding principle of equanimity is very much
linked to the quality of our love. Consider, for a moment, the
relationship between children and their parents. When children are small, their parents show great compassion for their
hurts and sufferings as the children have difficulty communicating and fending for themselves. Later, as children grow up,
they learn to walk, talk, and gain many new abilities. During
this period, parents show love, support, joy, and enthusiasm
for their children's achievements. Once children become fully
grown and are living on their own, however, parents have
another choice to make: between interference or letting go,
between possession or freedom.

As a noninterfering parent, you let your grown child
act according to his or her own wish and personal discre-
tion. This is a process of putting your own preferences aside.

It is an acceptance of the fact that each generation sees and experiences life a little differently than the one before. Equanimity does not mean you no longer care about or love your children, or anyone else for that matter. Instead, you love and empower them more fully, free of clinging and expectation.

Do you impose an expectation upon your child, spouse, or loved one? Maybe it involves their following in your footsteps, becoming a professional in some field, or even fulfilling your own unrealized dreams? I wonder how many children are pushed to become beauty-pageant contestants or doctors at a young age? This kind of ongoing expectation can dampen joy in others. Yet too many parents—or lovers—cannot fully let go like this. As a result their love is stilted and mixed with their own needs and desires. Thich Nhat Hanh, in his book *The Heart of the Buddha's Teaching*, writes,

> A summer breeze can be very refreshing; but if we try to put it in a tin can so we can have it entirely for ourselves, the breeze will die. Our beloved is the same. He is like a cloud, a breeze, a flower. If you imprison him in a tin can, he will die. Yet many people do just that. They rob their loved one of his liberty, until he can no longer be himself.[2]

Experience: *What Is It Like to Be Loved by Me?*

How controlling is your love? How possessive? In this three-part experience, you learn what it is like to be loved by someone such as yourself. You will begin by stepping out of your own shoes and into those of someone you love deeply. This could be your child, parent, friend, spouse, or life partner. What is it like for them to receive your love? For this exercise, you will want to find a quiet place to sit and focus on your breathing. When you are centered, begin to reflect in the following way.

Begin by imagining yourself as your loved one. Feel what that is like. Feel into this person's particular sensitivities and needs. Try not to pull back or analyze too deeply. Let yourself feel this person in ways you probably never have —from his or her being. Of course, it can be helpful to follow up later and have a conversation with your loved one about your experience of stepping into his or her shoes to see if you were even close! What is important is that you make an effort to experience where you have equanimity in your loving relationship.

When you are ready, have your imagined loved one answer the following questions: What is the quality of love that (your name here) gives me? Is it full or limited? Where does this love seek to limit my freedom? Where does it fail to see and appreciate the real me? How and when does it leave me feeling frustrated or empty?

Let yourself reflect on what comes into your mind. If you find that your love is constricting in some way, do not get ready to jump in with blame. Instead, congratulate yourself on uncovering something of great importance! Use this newfound knowledge, however subtle it may be, to undo patterns of control and possession that may have undermined your relationships. Let yourself be guided to love in an empowering way.

The second part of this experience lets you step into your own shoes to ask these same questions of your parents, spouse, or others who matter deeply. What can you do if you discover patterns of control that are upsetting? First and foremost, remember that you can show equanimity and a peaceful respect for these persons. After all, they may not be aware of how they are impacting you. In addition, you can use your newfound understanding of others' need to possess by looking at your own decision-making process. Perhaps you can become more confident in making decisions for yourself, rather than pleasing others.

Finally, you will remain in your own shoes as you seek to answer, What is it like for me to be loved by me? Take a deep breath before you begin. Ask the same questions as before. The answers you receive can be very revealing. Perhaps you will find there is an inner critic who demands a lot for his or her love. Or you may discover that there are other controls and limitations placed on how much you can love yourself— on which parts of you can get love and which parts cannot. Try not to censor anything. At the same time, bring your sense of equanimity to play on all you experience. Share this openness and acceptance with your inner critic or any other parts that need it. Let yourself love yourself more freely without limitation and expectation. May you find this experience liberating enough to let unencumbered love flow into your life and your relationships.

Principle 10: *Loving-Kindness*

The ancients knew something which we seem to have forgotten.

—Albert Einstein

By nature I tend to be a skeptic. Having been raised in a family that shifted between atheism and agnosticism, I took to the spiritual path later in life. My father, an engineer, regarded everything as a scientist might: if it was not observable, then it was not real. It seems I adopted this family trait and cultural thought pattern, despite having had several mystical experiences throughout my life. For some reason I just could not break the irrational hold of my rational mind.

Then, one sunny day in Southern California, I was invited to join some friends who were having lunch with a spiritual teacher about whom I had heard. Over a wonderful meal of Japanese food, we discussed our various creative projects, and then we walked back to my friends' office. When it was time to say good bye, I prepared to shake hands with the spiritual teacher. Instead, he wrapped a big, warm bear hug around me, and I reciprocated. Instantly, I felt something subtle, something unusual, that I could not put into words. For a few brief moments we stood like this and then parted, wishing each other well.

As I turned to leave the room it happened. A tingling as sweet as honey spilled warmly down my back and neck, soon covering my entire body. My being felt like it had been immersed in the energy of pure love, as if an inner light had been switched on. As this giddy sensation filled me with an overwhelming sense of joy and well-being, I could not suppress the wide smile that spread across my face. At the same time, I was grateful toward this caring spiritual teacher, as well as toward all others.

This was, I sensed instantly, the energy of loving-kindness that I had been practicing and had learned from other teachers. Now I knew what it felt like. More importantly, I knew with absolute certainty that it was *real*, as real and powerful as the juice in an electrical outlet. And it could be transmitted by anyone willing to practice it, just like the Buddha had taught more than 2,500 years ago.

OPENING THE DOOR
TO LOVING-KINDNESS

True loving-kindness, or *metta paramita*, knows no boundaries. This ancient principle shows no discrimination or favoritism. Prime examples of loving-kindness are found in stories of how Jesus, Buddha, and Mohammed all fed the hungry and starving, without discrimination. Loving-kindness is the love between friends. Sometimes, it is depicted as a refusal to harm others even though they wish us harm. The Jataka tales—Buddhist stories that teach various virtues—describe a lifetime when Buddha was born as a snake. Even as a venomous reptile, he displayed loving-kindness by refusing to bite the snake charmer who captured and killed him.

We all need love. Love is the basic glue that brings us together as people and beings that coexist on this planet and in the cosmos. As babies we need love. We need it as experimenting adolescents and thriving adults. We need it when we prepare to die. When love and approval are withheld, withdrawn, or conditional, then we search other ways to get it—some good, some bad. Even war puts a perverse twist on how to attain love. After all, do people not fight in wars for the love of their supreme deity or the love of their country? Why else would humans choose to fight and kill others when they could just as easily try to love and understand them?

Still, loving-kindness does not mean you let anyone abuse you. If that were the case, then you would not be showing *yourself* very much love and compassion. A woman I know, Susan, works at a retail establishment. When she discovered that a fellow employee was openly stealing, she could have looked the other way. Even though she did not want the employee to suffer and lose his job, she felt that reporting the theft was an act of loving-kindness—toward the store, the employee, and herself.

On the other hand, if Susan had ignored the theft—out of what she might have considered to be love and compassion—then she would have only been deceiving herself. If she had ignored it, the employee would have continued stealing. Other employees might have observed this, too, and decided that theft was acceptable. Inevitably, store profit would plummet. Some people, even innocent ones, might lose their jobs or have their hours cut in an effort to bolster profit. Product prices might rise, too, which would punish the innocent customer. By saying nothing, Susan would have stolen from herself and others. Her decision to be truthful was an expression of loving-kindness for herself and others—without deception. As Danish philosopher and theologian Søren Kierkegaard eloquently said, "To cheat oneself out of love is the most terrible deception; it is an eternal loss for which there is no reparation, either in time or in eternity."[1]

There is no one, according to this ancient principle, who is unworthy of receiving loving-kindness. This kind of love, however, is at odds with our normally accepted prejudices and conditions about love. Usually, we tend to love a person who reciprocates by making us feel good in some way—be it familial love, romantic love, or nostalgic love. Personal and worldly love picks favorites, according to our likes and dislikes.

Loving-kindness, however, goes beyond all the forms of worldly love. While it may be true that the love of a mother and father is unconditional, parents feel that way for *their* children—the ones to whom they have an emotional attachment—not necessarily for others'. But what if we could feel that same selfless and open love toward all? Jesus taught a revolutionary kind of loving-kindness when he declared, "You have heard that it was said, 'Love your neighbor and hate your enemy.' But I tell you: Love your enemies and pray for those who persecute you" (Matt. 5:43–44). He also said, "Love your neighbor as yourself" (Matt. 19:19).

Jesus' approach to love is worth examining because it forces us to think about the question "How should I love myself so that I might know how to love a neighbor, friend, enemy, or anyone else?" The answer is extraordinarily simple: it begins with forgiveness.

While forgiveness is not specifically one of the Buddha's ancient principles, it might as well be. For without it, patience, equanimity, and loving-kindness would ring hollow. Forgiveness is the first step in loving ourselves. Why? It is one thing to suspend judgment. It is quite another to offer forgiveness. When someone harms us, we may feel pain and anger. We may even desire retribution, conveniently forgetting the consequences. Forgiveness, however, short-circuits the cycle of suffering by recognizing that all beings have hurt others in some way. We are all subject to frailty, subject to acting selfishly. At some point in our lives, have we not all either been hurt by others or hurt others? Is not life filled with struggle, disappointment, and loss for both the king and the pauper? This mutual condition is the great equalizer. Fortunately, we are equally capable of forgiving ourselves and others. Forgiveness is like a healing and purifying substance that absorbs and transforms anger, self-righteousness, and other unhealthy emotions. By doing so we open the door to grace and loving-kindness.

Yet forgiveness is frequently misunderstood. First, it is important to recognize that forgiving does not erase the harmful behavior or abuses of others. And the act of forgiving does not—and should not—condone these abuses or in any way allow them to be repeated. If forgiving allowed abuse to continue, then it would be misguided. Forgiving does not mean that anyone should suffer again. It does mean this: that you care about the well-being of those who suffer, even as they hurt others. This is compassion. It is also loving-kindness, understanding, wisdom, and patience.

Forgiving, like the other ancient principles, begins at home. Do you have a problem forgiving yourself? If you constantly blame yourself, how can you hope to forgive others? Again, family patterns can be revealing. My own grandmother, for instance, proudly boasted that she had never said the words "I'm sorry." Does your family have a "clan wave" that persists from generation to generation? You do not have to slavishly follow along the road others have walked. There are other more beneficial and liberating paths, and forgiveness is one with the power to mend and heal.

When it comes to forgiveness, I am always reminded of Oscar Wilde's humorous and poignant remark that "the most parents can hope for is to live long enough for their children to forgive them." How many of us take anger with us to our graves? There is no need to wait for your parents to grow older. Forgive them today, now, this instant. So long as you hold onto the victim's anger, you are the victim.

The Buddha made the point that hate does not overcome hate. Only love and forgiveness can overcome the anger you or anyone feels at having been harmed or abused. If you are unable to forgive right now, do not force it. Let it spring from truth and knowing within your heart. Surely, there is some old flame, business partner, or family member whom you wronged—either intentionally or unintentionally. Would it not be wonderful to be forgiven? There is a wise old saying in the East that says, "We come into this world without any enemies, and it is best to leave this world the same way."

So, now, let yourself be that parent, for example, who knows you have wronged your children and yet hope for the grace of forgiveness. Think of someone you have hurt as you reflect on the words below. Allow forgiveness to act as a salve for your wounded spirit so that you may let go and move on.

> May I forgive myself for hurting others.
> May others forgive me for hurting them.
> May I forgive myself for hurting myself.
> May my words, thoughts, and deeds follow the path of
>   divine [or name of supreme deity] will.

By sending forgiveness, you also open the gateway to a more awakened and sensitive behavior—alert to even the subtle consequences of your actions and thoughts. Jesus speaks to this in the Bible (Luke 6:37) when he says:

Do not judge, and you will not be judged.
Do not condemn, and you will not be condemned.
Forgive, and you will be forgiven.

LOVE IS ACTION

Love is not just a positive thought or emotion. It is a very real action that attends to your most primary survival needs. For example, if you are severely sick and suffering, what conceivable comfort can you offer to another? That is why it is not possible to "love your neighbor as yourself" unless you love yourself enough to care for your own physical well-being and security. This means you need to lovingly care for the body that has been placed in your safekeeping. You need to provide it with the right kinds of wholesome nourishment (for mind, body, and spirit) so that it can grow and achieve the ideal health for which it is so beautifully designed and intended.

I know of a man, Ted, who made some unusual choices about what he put in his body. At a restaurant once, instead of ordering an "extra lean" corned beef sandwich, he asked for one with "extra fat." I will never forget the stunned and perplexed expression on that waitress's face. This kind of indulgence might be understandable if done rarely or if combined with regular exercise. But in Ted's case it was not.

How do you care for your body? I am often amazed to

see how little regard some people have for the vehicle of their consciousness. Some do a much better job of washing and maintaining their cars! Perhaps this is why traditional Buddhist loving-kindness practice often begins with the following blessing:

May I be well.

This does not mean we have to wait or pray for something outside of ourselves to make us well. We must do it because this is one way to love ourselves. While in the monastery during a retreat, I met an extraordinary man, Maurice, who had lived for more than two years with an inoperable brain tumor. Even with chemotherapy, his doctor had given him only months to live. When I asked Maurice how he had managed to stay well, he responded, "I'm not waiting for Buddha or anyone else to help me. I'm helping myself." I am proud to know someone who takes his well-being so seriously and responsibly.

The loving-kindness blessing continues:

May I be happy.
May I be at peace.
May I be free from pain, hunger, and suffering.

In addition to physical well-being, we need to nourish ourselves with deep emotional happiness and contentment. You will not be able to "love your neighbor" if you are emotionally distraught and filled with angst. You can, however, live in the moment, rather than in the emotions of the past (guilt) or future (worry). You can be thankful for what is in your life at this very moment.

You can also find happiness by examining those sources

and excesses of craving and attachment that cause you conflict, stress, and anxiety. This may take time, but whenever
you patiently resist the urge to gossip, to feel ill will toward
others, or to do something injurious to your health, you will
gain greater emotional strength and stability. In addition, it is
important to cultivate inner happiness through the right kind
of skillful action—in the choice of friends, associations, and
work. All these are positive, generous actions that you can
take on behalf of your own well-being at all levels.

On the other hand, you can assume the qualities mentioned in an article called "How to Drive Yourself Crazy" by
Dorothy Harrison, Ph.D. This article has been adapted and
posted on several inspirational Internet sites. Tips for driving
yourself crazy include such things as "save your major worries until about midnight," "keep an inventory of your faults,"
"set unreasonable goals," "put off everything until the last
minute," "never trust anyone," and "above all, never seek
help." To these I would like to add, "Be completely selfish,
being careful to never show love or compassion to anyone. In
this way you can add to the world's misery and live a completely lonely and unfulfilled existence!"

THE DIVINE ABODES

What actually is loving-kindness? The Buddha's discourse on loving-kindness, as translated by Gil Fronsdal in
Teachings of the Buddha, shows that loving-kindness is not found
in any one thing, but in all:

This is the work of those who are skilled and peaceful,
who seek the good:

May they be able and upright, straightforward, of gentle
   speech and not proud.
May they be content and easily supported, unburdened,
   with their senses calmed.
May they be wise, not arrogant and without desire for
   the possessions of others.
May they do nothing mean or that the wise would
   reprove.

May all beings be happy.
May they live in safety and joy.
All living beings, whether weak or strong, tall, stout, av-
   erage or short, seen or unseen, near or distant, born or
   to be born, may they all be happy.

Let no one deceive another or despise any being in any
state, let none by anger or hatred wish harm to another.

As a mother watches over her child, willing to risk her
own life to protect her only child, so with a boundless
heart should one cherish all living beings, suffusing the
whole world with unobstructed loving-kindness.

Standing or walking, sitting or lying down, during all
one's waking hours, may one remain mindful of this heart
and this way of living that is the best in the world.[2]

Another way to experience and understand loving-kindness is through what are known in Buddhism as the "Divine
Abodes" or "Four Immeasurables." Here, loving-kindness is
experienced as the four inseparable elements of love, compassion, sympathy of joy, and equanimity. Of these four, only
sympathy of joy has not been explicitly mentioned thus far.

So, what is it?

Sympathy of joy is the happiness we feel when someone else succeeds or gains happiness. Sometimes, though, sympathetic joy can be hard to come by. Suppose, for example, that my friend gets the job I always desired, but was denied. If I believe that my friend's gain is my loss, then I am only devaluing my worth as a person and cannot feel joy. This will be the case so long as I put myself on a scale to see how various parts of me measure up. The problem with this approach is that there will always be someone who has *more* in some category. Instead of being envious or jealous, however, I could choose to be deeply joyful for my friend's empowerment—whether in relationships, work, or personal fulfillment.

Sympathetic joy cannot coexist with envy, greed, and competition. You will know that your experience of sympathetic joy is lacking if you are always comparing what you want or have with what someone else has. Does your car/house/clothing/jewelry/job always have to be "nicer," "bigger," "better," "faster," "more expensive," or "more prestigious"? This is a sure formula for misery.

Sympathetic joy, on the other hand, lets us share in the good fortune of others—free from holding onto ill feelings. Of course, there may be times that someone gloats and brags. Does this mean we must be joyful even when someone else is arrogant? Actually, this may be the very time to have compassionate love and understanding. Here is an opportunity to be understanding of how another's arrogance, envy, or jealousy is a sign of suffering. Just as importantly, reacting negatively may keep our hearts constricted and our minds attached to harmful emotions. By not taking another's action personally, we can learn to grow our compassion and support for others under more and more trying circumstances.

Sympathy of joy, then, is a vital complement to love, compassion, and equanimity. In another sense, these Four Immeasurables can be thought of as expressing immeasurable love that, above all else, recognizes another's innermost being. Here is found a mother's unconditional love, a friend's joyful and compassionate love, a lover's unfettered love, a child's boundless love, and a spiritual teacher's nonjudgmental love.

By experiencing immeasurable love you become part of the heart flow that sustains the world through creativity and healing. The Buddha himself said that the Divine Abodes were a path to awakening. Dwell in this abode of love, and you will bring immeasurable change into your life. This energy is here with you, in your heart and being. Reflect on loving-kindness now or when you have some moments to sit in quietude.

Experience: *Loving-Kindness Practice*

Sit in silence, focused on your breathing. When you are centered, begin by forgiving yourself for the hurts you may have caused others. If you have difficulty forgiving yourself as you are today, picture yourself as a young child or baby. (Some people find it easier to forgive this small, innocent self they once were.) Now send loving-kindness to yourself as you repeat:

> May I be well.
> May I be happy.
> May I be at peace.
> May I live long.
> May I be free from pain, hunger, and suffering.

Repeat this blessing as many times as necessary, letting the feeling of love enter your being and heart. Continue until the image of yourself is immersed in light, radiant, smiling, and filled with unlimited, immeasurable love. If you cannot feel this love, *please do not blame yourself.* Loving-kindness takes time, so be patient. Love is not a goal you are trying to achieve. It is a better approach to life that takes some getting used to.

Now, you will begin expanding the love outward. Begin by imagining your wise teachers or guides. If none come to mind, you can envision Jesus, Buddha, or another historical figure whom you admire. As you see each person in your mind's eye, repeat the following words, either aloud or mentally:

> May my teacher [or use name] be well.
> May [name] be happy.
> May [name] be at peace.
> May [he/she] live long.
> May [he/she] be free from pain, hunger, and suffering.

You will repeat this sequence five more times in the following order: once for family, once for friends, once for neutral persons, once for those who are unfriendly, and once for all beings. For neutral persons, this could be anyone you have seen during the day whom you do not really know. Some loving-kindness practices use the word *enemies* for the next group, although I prefer the phrase "those who are unfriendly."

> May [name] be well.
> May [name] be happy.
> May [name] be at peace.
> May [he/she] live long.
> May [he/she] be free from pain, hunger, and suffering.

When you are finished, place your hands at your heart center and dedicate your blessings for all. Do not be surprised if you feel some strong emotions during this practice. Opening to love means opening yourself to the world's suffering as well. If you begin to cry, do not force yourself to stop, but rest in equanimity and compassion so you are not overcome by your feelings. This practice is so important that many monks and laity do it daily. You certainly do not have to be a monk to experience the benefits!

THE LOVING-KINDNESS HEADLINES

Too often, the news headlines fixate on the world's difficulties, chasms, and violence. Realistically, shouldering these burdens will not likely alter anything—other than degrade our own mental, physical, and spiritual well-being. I am not saying to ignore them, but hatred and prejudice can be like a contagious disease. On the other hand, there are just as many headlines for loving-kindness out there if we will just look for them. Best of all, we can choose to create our own headlines—actively changing the world for the better.

For example, soft-spoken Irene works in a grocery-store chain. When she is diagnosed with cancer, Irene needs to undergo treatment with chemotherapy. Knowing she will have to miss several days' work, she is prepared to turn in her sick days and time off in order to accommodate the treatment and recovery period. Her coworkers, though, do not see it that way. They fill in for her—allowing Irene to retain a vacation and take days off as needed without losing pay.

In Chicago, Illinois, Rita prepares for a badly needed vacation away from frigid winter weather and a hectic schedule of rounds as a neurologist specializing in geriatric patients. But instead of flying south for a week in the sun, she travels to her old college town in Illinois. There she will care for an old college friend, Gary, who suffers from post–polio syndrome and spends 90 percent of his time on a ventilator. For Rita, Gary is an inspiration because he refuses to be restricted by his body's limitations and leads a full life. Rita's act of love and compassion is the gift of a special friendship. It is also a gift to Gary's spouse, who badly needs time away to recharge her own batteries and have a rare visit with family members from out of town.

Andrew, in his fifties, is a tenured professor at a university in Asia. But his life turns upside down when he learns that his son, who lives back in the States, has landed in prison. Andrew and his wife make what is a joint family decision. He gives up his job and moves back to the United States to be close to his son. For Andrew, this is not about sacrificing his future security; neither is it about rescuing his son. There is no question about whether he is doing the right thing, for, as Andrew says, "I am doing what is best for me: that is, showing my love for the people I care most for in the world."

As these stories illustrate, there is an endless number of ways to spread loving-kindness. Eventually, we can expand our loving-kindness from friend and family to include neighbors, people we do not know, and even those who may be unfriendly toward us. Imagine how your loving-kindness headlines will read. Write them down in a journal and manifest them. Or write them down after you do an act of loving-kindness. Here are a few examples:

"Man Calls Animal Shelter for Lost Dog"
"Woman Invites Lonely Neighbor for Dinner"
"Loving-Kindness Breaks Out at Picnic"
"Man Stops Criticizing for an Hour"
"Forty-Year-Old Woman Forgives Neglectful Mother"
"Husband and Wife Volunteer for Hospice Work"

"Woman Flosses Regularly, Improves Health"

What is important is that you are awake to your experience of loving-kindness—however it may be felt. Each awake moment will light your spiritual lamp that much more brightly.

Experience: *The Universal Smile*

During a private session with my teacher U Silananda, I once asked him how he maintained his health. Though in his seventies at the time, he was filled with a vibrancy and joy of someone many years younger. His answer was simple and direct. First, he ate wholesome food in the right quantities (using moderation to eat neither too much nor too little). Second, he took frequent walks (recommended by the Buddha). Third, he inwardly thanked his body and all its individual parts with love each morning. Some traditions call this practice the "Inner Smile" or the "Universal Smile." Here is how it works.

Each morning when you awaken (or evening before you sleep), center your mind on your body's presence. Take a deep breath and feel your diaphragm move. Feel how marvelous it is that each breath fills your lungs, sends oxygen to your muscles and organs, and sustains you. You may want to wiggle your toes and feel how effortlessly they follow your command. Take a few moments to feel grateful for this body, this extraordinary gift that you possess.

Now, starting at your feet and working your way up to your head, place your attention on each part of your body. For example, you can begin by focusing on your feet. As you do this, acknowledge how your feet have been masterfully constructed to help you walk and carry your weight. Picture them from the inside, filled with muscles, tendons, and bones, all working in concert. Feel a sense of gratitude and thankfulness to them. You may even visualize them filling up with light, being energized and well. You may even wish to say the words, "May my feet be well and in full and perfect health; may they continue to help me along my path."

You can continue this sequence for scanning various body parts, especially the heart, kidneys, liver, spine, and brain, as well as other sense organs that assist in your well-being. Feel your connection to each of these parts that help to make a joyful and fulfilling life possible. If any part of your body is injured or needs healing, ask that it may be healed. Send to it your love and appreciation for all it has done for you thus far. If you have hurt it in some way because of neglect or abuse, forgive yourself and ask your body to forgive you. You need to know that your physical body wants to support your spiritual goals. That is what it is here for!

When you have completed the Inner Smile practice by addressing all your body, let yourself rest for a moment in the presence of it. Give thanks and ask for your body to guide you in doing what is best for it. By now, you will really be smiling and ready to face the day (or night, as the case may be). This is a wonderful ancient practice that will help you find the strength to do what is right for your body—and the rest of you.

During the day, be more aware of your body. It really will let you know when it is happy and when it is not. I know several people, for example, who have told me that they feel less energetic when they drink too much caffeine. It is easy to make corrections if you take the time to become good friends with your body.

MANTRAS FOR LOVE AND HEALING

The spiritual practice of using mantras has been around for thousands of years. Among Hindu literature, the earliest Vedic hymns give mantra a legacy dating from 1500 B.C. The recitation of these hymns by Hindu priests probably adds another two thousand years of oral history to spiritual practices using sound, word, and music. Still, there are many misconceptions about this essential spiritual tool—what it really is and what it can do.

Even today, journalists routinely misinterpret the word *mantra*. It seems that every week there is a story in TV or print news that describes any terse, repetitive, and unchanging statement by a public figure—from sports to politics—as that person's "mantra." Of course, that could not be farther from the truth.

In my Sanskrit dictionary, for example, mantra is defined as "a sacred word or phrase of spiritual significance and power," and "sacred utterances."[3] Derived from its Sanskrit root of *man*, which means "to think," mantra refers to a sound, word, or phrase containing spiritual essence or sacred power. In its most fundamental and elemental form, a mantra is sound—including primal sounds, syllables, words, or phrases that express the absolute reality or invoke the Divine. For this reason, mantras are sometimes referred to as tools of the mind and instruments of liberation. Training in mantra is important for another reason. It teaches us to respect the power of words and how to use all words and language in a soft, gentle, thoughtful, kind, and beneficial way.

How do mantras work? Fundamentally, they possess vibrational energy that moves through all levels of physical and spiritual being. Further, many believe that this sound energy of mantras corresponds to the body's chakra points, which gives mantra its unique ability to transform and manifest changes within, as well as outside of, the body. One of the primary techniques associated with mantra is repetition. Like a transmitter, repetition increases the strength and reach of a mantra's signal.

Sacred word can also carry a well-meant intention or purpose. Intention charges your chakras and transmits energy into the field of the interconnected universe. This is where mantra's potential for infinite organizing power comes into being, whether transmitting harmony, well-being, health, and blessings, or generating meaningful events. Remember, however, that a wish or a dream for something—like winning the lottery—may be only another kind of craving and attachment.

When you create an intention, take care that it is direct, honest, and clear. While there are mantras for almost everything—from finding a loving relationship and healing to creating abundance—what manifests also depends on your subconscious thoughts. Consciously, you might want a relationship, but if you subconsciously feel undeserving, then the mantra will not bring satisfactory results. I also believe that one of the factors that makes an intention successful is whether or not it serves more than just a self-serving need. In this way, you stay true to the core of living kindness.

One area where we have evidence of all this is in how prayer can be used to heal. We have all heard about stories of miraculous or spontaneous healing, accomplished either by healers or by prayer. I personally know of one case where a woman with inoperable cancer was healed with the help of a monk who prayed for her—from a distance of several hundred miles away—every morning for a half an hour, while she prayed at the same time. For Larry Dossey, M.D., author of *Healing Words*, this kind of healing is not so unusual. According to Dossey,

The most practical reason to examine prayer in healing is simply that at least some of the time, *it works*. The evidence is simply overwhelming that prayer functions at a distance to change physical processes in a variety of organisms, from bacteria to humans. These data . . . are so impressive that I have come to regard them as among the best-kept secrets in medical science.[4]

This use of prayer is not really new. Traditionally, mantra was an important tool for restoring health, and ancient Vedic healers often used it in their healing rituals. In fact, these healers had such skillful ability to cure snakebites—partly through the chanting of medicinal hymns from Hindu scripture—that Alexander of Macedonia kept several Indian healers by his side!

Yet as good as the evidence is, prayer does not always work—at least not in the way we might think it should. This leads us to ask an important question: If prayer truly is an effective therapy, why does it not deliver more consistent results? First, let us remember that there is not any single antibiotic that cures all illnesses. Each mode of therapy has a specific ability and, even then, requires help from our unique immune systems.

So at present, there may be no simple answer to this question—we need to accept that as spiritual beings with physical bodies, no two of us possess the identical equipment or antennas for either receiving or sending spiritual energy through sacred words. For example, the space-based Hubble Telescope—with no interference from the atmosphere—collects images with greater clarity than much larger telescopes on Earth. Still, it is comforting to know that sacred words exist out there (and in here), beaming their messages in all directions. And the fact that prayer works at all shows that we are wired to receive and send a field of conscious energy capable of altering our world and ourselves—maybe even across time and space.

Most importantly, however, living kindness means recognizing and accepting that sacred word does not come with a guarantee of getting healed, finding love, or buying the winning lottery ticket. Always there is the element of faith, which is a way of letting go of expectations and attachments. We do not truly know what is the "highest good" for each person. What is more, what *we* want for them may not be it. In this way we trust in the process, aware that the Divine's ways are often beyond our knowing. If our telescope is smudged, well, maybe it is supposed to be that way! Still, we can clean the surface through effort and commitment, at the same time nourishing the spirit that is inseparable from our being.

The most universally recognized sacred sound is probably *aum*, or *om*—the mystical, cosmic sound of creation. This sound encompasses the all, the one manifestation of absolute truth. According to the ancient Hindu Upanishads, all words are thought to be variations of om's primal sound. So rather than being simply a word, *om* represents the manifestation of truth underlying all realities.

Use of the cosmic sound *om* as a mantra, though, is not limited to Hinduism. Not only has it been adopted for use in some Buddhist mantras, it is now used to bring people of many faiths together. In fact, it is used in a very important mantra that you can use with your loving-kindness practice:

Om mani padme hung
(pronounced "om mah-nee pahd-may oong")

This mantra, which translates as "The jewel is in the lotus," is perhaps one of the most well-known mantras for transmitting love and compassion to others. It is the mantra of Avalokitesvara, known as the Buddha of Compassion. There are stories of Tibetan lamas who spent their lives repeating this mantra to every living being they ever encountered. It is a powerful and overwhelming mantra that will not only charge your heart with loving energy, but make it more expansive, caring, and accepting, too.

This blessing can be used anytime, even at mealtime. I often like to repeat it mentally while eating. In this way I can transmit loving-kindness on behalf of all beings so that everyone may have enough to eat. If you think more about the meaning, try to visualize where a lotus comes from—out of the muddy water. Yet here it is, emerging from the depths and opening its petals to the sunlight. In the same way, you can open the jewels of your gentle heart and awakened consciousness to others.

If you are musically inclined, you may want to chant this mantra. What is the difference between mantra and chant? Chant is the singing of sacred words. The methods and styles of chant vary from tradition to tradition and can be very specialized. Typically, chants are applied in one of three basic ways: to repeat a mantra, to recite scripture or doctrine, or to pray and say blessings. The chanting of protective *suttas* mentioned earlier is an example of chanting to give blessings, as well as to recite Buddhist teachings.

As Don Campbell points out in *The Mozart Effect*, his landmark book about the healing power of music, even nonsensical sounds are soothing when repeated. "Thus," writes Campbell, "chanting can be effective whether the words have meaning or not—whether one repeats *Om mani padme hum* in the Tibetan Buddhist canon or *shaboom, shaboom, ya, da, da, da, da, shaboom, shaboom* in the sacred Motown tradition!"[5]

TODAY WE CAN

Loving-kindness is one of the great marvels and mysteries of the universe. I believe that one day the science behind this powerful healing energy will be quantified. In the meantime, we possess the capability to use it, to know it, and to feel it. Its purpose is clear, so why wait?

Practice and experience this wonder of wonders *today*. Who knows what tomorrow may bring? *Today we can* share the expansiveness in our own hearts. *Today we can* ease suffering. *Today we can* foster hope. *Today we can* energize the courage to care. *Today we can* . . .

Welcome to the Beginning

Though it seems that we have come to the end of exploring the guiding values, that is not so. We have really arrived at the beginning—of the rest of our lives applying and discovering the blessings offered by these principles. Imagine, for example, that you could gather together in one room all the most enlightened of priests, nuns, bishops, monks, rabbis, imams, lamas, Sufi masters, mystics, saints, and shamans. Other than having one heck of a blissful party, it is doubtful they would agree on things like the precise nature of the Divine or what happens after death. However, let them discuss what it takes to live a good and beneficial life, and they would more than likely reach an accord based on principles. Or perhaps they would not discuss the subject at all. Instead, they might just go out and experience it. And in the end, what more can anyone ask?

Though you may not always see them at your side, the living kindness principles are always present, just as the sun never stops shining and the wind never stops blowing. It is my hope that you experience the principles in every action you take.

Know them as compassionate friends whose wisdom you trust completely. Love them for their constant effort and gentle

support on your behalf. Rest in the healing grace of their lim-
itless patience, wisdom, equanimity, and forgiveness. Let their
ever-present simplicity and ethics guide and fortify you in difficult times. Feel them as you would a mother's boundless
generosity, loving-kindness, and caring discipline. Worry not
when you seem to lose them because they are truthful and
resolute about never stranding you in time of crisis. Neither
will they make unreasonable demands or judge you harshly.

In closing, my own hope is this:

May you find all blessings, and may all blessings find
    you.
May you experience the joy of living kindness manifest
    in each moment and each being.
May you use living kindness as a healing force for peace.

Notes

Note: All quotations in Living Kindness *not documented here are from the author's personal collection acquired from a variety of sources but containing no specific reference information.*

Introduction: *Touchstones for the Spirit*

1. U Silananda, trans., *Paritta Pali and Protective Suttas* (Daly City, CA: Dhammananda Vihara, 1995), 11–13.

2. As quoted in Kay Redfield Jamison, *An Unquiet Mind* (New York: Vintage Books, 1995), 146.

3. Lama Surya Das, *Awakening the Buddha Within: Tibetan Wisdom for the Western World* (New York: Broadway Books, 1997), 17.

4. Thomas Byrom, trans., *Dhammapada: Sayings of the Buddha* (Boston: Shambhala, 1993), 55.

5. From a speech given by Ken McLeod at Dharma Rain Zen Center, Portland, OR, 2001.

6. J. Krishnamurti, *The Book of Life* (New York: HarperCollins, 1995), 123.

Guideposts

1. Jack Kornfield, *After the Ecstasy, the Laundry* (New York: Bantam Books, 2000), 207–208.

2. Ananda Maitreya, trans., *Dhammapada: The Path of Truth* (Berkeley: Parallax Press, 1995), 51.

3. Thich Nhat Hahn, *Cultivating the Mind of Love* (Berkeley: Parallax Press, 1996), 67–68.

Principle 1: *Generosity*

1. Rupert Sheldrake, *The Rebirth of Nature* (Rochester, VT: Park Street Press, 1994), 143.

2. From a speech given by the Dalai Lama in Portland, OR, May 2001.

3. Rabbi Bradley Bleefeld and Robert Shook, trans., *Saving the World Entire* (New York: Plume, 1998), 167–168.

4. Gordon Hinckley, *Standing for Something* (New York: Three Rivers Press, 2000), 106.

5. Jack Kornfield and Paul Breiter, eds., *A Still Forest Pool: The Insight Meditation of Achaan Chah* (Wheaton, IL: Quest Books, 1985), x.

6. M. K. Gandhi, *Vows and Observances* (Berkeley: Berkeley Hills Books, 1999), 133.

Principle 2: *Effort*

1. Thomas Merton, *New Seeds of Contemplation* (New York: New Directions, 1961), 29.

2. Thomas Byrom, trans., *Dhammapada: Sayings of the Buddha* (Boston: Shambhala, 1993), 96–97, 101.

3. Inayat Khan, *Notes from the Unstruck Music from the Gayan of Inayat Khan* (Tucson: Message Publications, 1985), 78.

4. Kalu Rinpoche, *The Dharma* (New York: State University of New York Press, 1986), 81.

5. Thomas Ashley-Farrand, *Healing Mantras* (New York: Ballantine Wellspring, 1999), 210.

6. Lama Surya Das, *Awakening the Buddha Within: Tibetan Wisdom for the Western World* (New York: Broadway Books, 1997), 143.

Principle 3: *Patience*

1. Jack Kornfield, ed. *Teachings of the Buddha*, trans. Bukkyo Dendo Kyokai (Boston: Shambhala, 1996), 96.

2. Lao Tzu, *The Way of Life*, trans. R. B. Blakney (New York: Mentor, 1983), 110.

3. Santideva, *A Guide to the Bodhisattva Way of Life*, trans. V. Wallace and B. Wallace (Ithaca, NY: Snow Lion Publications, 1997), 66.

4. Ibid., 69.

5. Saint Benedict, *The Rule of St. Benedict* (Collegeville, MN: The Liturgical Press, 1981), 94.

6. David Bohm, *On Dialogue* (New York: Routledge, 1996), 4.

Principle 4: *Ethics*

1. Padmasambhava, *Advice from the Lotus-Born*, trans. Erik Pema Kunsang (Hong Kong: Rangjung Yeshe Publications, 1994), 30.

2. M. K. Gandhi, *Vows and Observances* (Berkeley: Berkeley Hills Books, 1999), 9.

3. Donald Altman, *Art of the Inner Meal: The Power of Mindful Practices to Heal Our Food Cravings*, rev. ed. (Portland, OR: Moon Lake Media, 2002), 121–122.

4. Ananda Maitreya, trans., *Dhammapada: The Path of Truth* (Berkeley: Parallax Press, 1995), 23.

Principle 5: *Simplicity and Meditation*

1. Huntington and Smith, eds., *Emerson Day by Day* (New York: T. Y. Crowell & Co., 1905), 2.

2. Thomas Byrom, trans., *Dhammapada: Sayings of the Buddha* (Boston: Shambhala, 1993), 70–71.

3. From a speech given by Greg Crosby at Lewis and Clark College, Graduate School of Education, Portland, OR, October 2002.

4. Thomas Byrom, trans., *Dhammapada: Sayings of the Buddha* (Boston: Shambhala, 1993), 49–50.

5. David Bohm, *Unfolding Meaning* (New York: Routledge, 1985), 6.

6. Ananda Maitreya, trans., *Dhammapada: The Path of Truth* (Berkeley: Parallax Press, 1995), 10.

7. Jack Kornfield, ed. *Teachings of the Buddha*, trans. Nyanaponika Thera (Boston: Shambhala, 1996), 76.

8. Thomas Keating, *Open Mind, Open Heart* (New York: Continuum Publishing Co., 1997), 5.

9. Aryeh Kaplan, *Jewish Meditation* (New York: Schocken Books, 1985), 51–52.

Principle 6: *Wisdom*

1. Martin Palmer, trans., *The Book of Chuang Tzu* (London: Penguin Arkana, 1996), 137, 142.

2. Lama Surya Das, *The Snow Lion's Turquoise Mane* (New York: HarperCollins, 1992), 32.

3. Wes Nisker, *Crazy Wisdom* (Berkeley: Ten Speed Press, 1998), 201.

Principle 7: *Truthfulness*

1. William Shakespeare, *Hamlet*, in *A Treasury of the Theatre: An Anthology of Great Plays from Aeschylus to Eugene O'Neill*, trans. Burns Mantle and John Gassner (New York: Simon and Schuster, 1935), 1.3.

2. Thich Nhat Hanh, *The Heart of the Buddha's Teaching* (New York: Broadway Books, 1988), 89.

Principle 8: *Steadfastness*

1. Swami Prabhavananda and Christopher Isherwood, trans., *The Song of God: Bhagavad-Gita* (England: Mentor, 1972), 31.

2. Ibid., 35.

3. Huston Smith, *Forgotten Truth* (San Francisco: HarperSanFrancisco, 1985), 112.

4. Deepak Chopra, *How to Know God* (New York: Harmony Books, 2000), 12.

Principle 9: *Equanimity*

1. Buddhaghosa, *The Path of Purification (Visuddhimagga)*, trans. Bhikkhu Nanamoli (Kandy, Sri Lanka: Buddhist Publication Society, 1991).

2. Thich Nhat Hanh, *The Heart of the Buddha's Teaching* (New York: Broadway Books, 1988), 175.

Principle 10: *Loving-Kindness*

1. Søren Kierkegaard, *Works of Love*, trans. Howard and Edna Hong (New York: HarperTorchbooks, 1962), 23–24.

2. Jack Kornfield, ed. *Teachings of the Buddha*, trans. Gil Fronsdal (Boston: Shambhala, 1996), 5–6.

3. *A Concise Dictionary of Indian Philosophy*, rev. ed., s.v. "Mantra."

4. Larry Dossey, M.D., *Healing Words* (San Francisco: HarperSanFrancisco, 1994), 2.

5. Don Campbell, *The Mozart Effect* (New York: Avon Books, 1997), 112.

Bibliography and Recommended Reading

Altman, Donald. *Art of the Inner Meal: The Power of Mindful Practices to Heal Our Food Cravings*. Rev. ed. Portland, OR: Moon Lake Media, 2002.

Ashley-Farrand, Thomas. *Healing Mantras*. New York: Ballantine Wellspring, 1999.

Bhikkhu Buddhadasa. *Heartwood of the Bodhi Tree*. Boston: Wisdom Publications, 1994.

Bleefeld, Rabbi Bradley, and Robert Shook, trans. *Saving the World Entire*. New York: Plume, 1998.

Bohm, David. *On Dialogue*. New York: Routledge, 1996.

———. *Unfolding Meaning*. New York: Routledge, 1985.

Buddhaghosa. *The Path of Purification (Visuddhimagga)*. Translated by Bhikkhu Nanamoli. Kandy, Sri Lanka: Buddhist Publication Society, 1991.

Byrom, Thomas, trans. *Dhammapada: Sayings of the Buddha*. Boston: Shambhala, 1993.

Campbell, Don. *The Mozart Effect*. New York: Avon Books, 1997.

Chopra, Deepak. *How to Know God*. New York: Harmony Books, 2000.

Dempsey, Carol, and Russell Butkus, eds. *All Creation Is Groaning*. Collegeville, MN: The Liturgical Press, 1999.

Dossey, Larry, M.D. *Healing Words*. San Francisco: HarperSanFrancisco, 1994.

Easwaran, Eknath. *The Mantram Handbook*. Petaluma, CA: Nilgiri Press, 1977.

Gandhi, M. K. *Vows and Observances*. Berkeley: Berkeley Hills Books, 1999.

Hahn, Thich Nhat. *Cultivating the Mind of Love*. Berkeley: Parallax Press, 1996.

———. *The Heart of the Buddha's Teaching*. New York: Broadway Books, 1988.

Hinckley, Gordon. *Standing for Something*. New York: Three Rivers Press, 2000.

Huntington and Smith, eds. *Emerson Day by Day*. New York: T. Y. Crowell & Co., 1905.

Kalu Rinpoche. *The Dharma*. New York: State University of New York Press, 1986.

Kaplan, Aryeh. *Jewish Meditation*. New York: Schocken Books, 1985.

Keating, Thomas. *Open Mind, Open Heart*. New York: Continuum Publishing Co., 1997.

Khan, Inayat. *Notes from the Unstruck Music from the Gayan of Inayat Khan*. Tucson: Message Publications, 1985.

Kierkegaard, Søren. *Works of Love*. Translated by Howard and Edna Hong. New York: HarperTorchbooks, 1962.

Kornfield, Jack. *After the Ecstasy, the Laundry*. New York: Bantam Books, 2000.

Kornfield, Jack, ed. *Teachings of the Buddha*. Boston: Shambhala, 1996.

Kornfield, Jack, and Paul Breiter, eds. *A Still Forest Pool: The Insight Meditation of Achaan Chah*. Wheaton, IL: Quest Books, 1985.

Kraybill, Donald (author), and Lucian Niemeyer (photographer). *Old Order Amish*. Baltimore: Johns Hopkins University Press, 1993.

Krishnamurti, J. *The Book of Life*. New York: HarperCollins, 1995.

————. *Think on These Things*. New York: HarperPerennial, 1989.

Lama Surya Das. *Awakening the Buddha Within: Tibetan Wisdom for the Western World*. New York: Broadway Books, 1997.

————. *The Snow Lion's Turquoise Mane*. New York: HarperCollins, 1992.

Lao Tzu. *The Way of Life*. Translated by R. B. Blakney. New York: Mentor, 1983.

Mahasi Sayadaw. *Fundamentals of Vipassana Meditation*. Translated by Maung Tha Noe. Berkeley: Dhammachakka Meditation Center, 1991.

Maitreya, Ananda, trans. *Dhammapada: The Path of Truth*. Berkeley: Parallax Press, 1995.

McLeod, Ken. *Wake Up to Your Life*. San Francisco: HarperSanFrancisco, 2001.

Merton, Thomas. *Mystics and Zen Masters*. New York: Noonday Press, 1996.

————. *New Seeds of Contemplation*. New York: New Directions, 1961.

Nerburn, Kent. *Make Me an Instrument of Your Peace*. San Francisco: HarperSanFrancisco, 1999.

Nikhilananda, Swami, trans. *The Gospel of Sri Ramakrishna*. New York: Ramakrishna-Vivekananda Center, 1958.

Nisker, Wes. *Crazy Wisdom*. Berkeley: Ten Speed Press, 1998.

Padmasambhava. *Advice from the Lotus-Born*. Translated by Erik Pema Kunsang. Hong Kong: Rangjung Yeshe Publications, 1994.

Palmer, Martin, trans. *The Book of Chuang Tzu*. London: Penguin Arkana, 1996.

Prabhavananda, Swami, and Christopher Isherwood, trans. *The Song of God: Bhagavad-Gita*. England: Mentor, 1972.

Redfield Jamison, Kay. *An Unquiet Mind*. New York: Vintage Books, 1995.

Rogers, Pattiann. *Firekeeper*. Minneapolis: Milkweed Editions, 1994.

Rumi, Jelaluddin. *Birdsong: Fifty-Three Short Poems*. Translated by Coleman Barks. Athens, GA: Maypop, 1993.

Saint Benedict. *The Rule of St. Benedict*. Collegeville, MN: The Liturgical Press, 1981.

Sangharakshita. *The Bodhisattva Ideal*. Birmingham, England: Windhorse Publications, 1999.

Santideva. *A Guide to the Bodhisattva Way of Life*. Translated by V. Wallace and B. Wallace. Ithaca, NY: Snow Lion Publications, 1997.

Sheldrake, Rupert. *The Rebirth of Nature*. Rochester, VT: Park Street Press, 1994.

Smith, Huston. *Forgotten Truth*. San Francisco: HarperSanFrancisco, 1985.

U Silananda. *Four Foundations of Mindfulness*. Boston: Wisdom Publications, 1990.

U Silananda, trans. *Paritta Pali and Protective Suttas*. Daly City, CA: Dhammananda Vihara, 1995.

Vajiranana Mahathera, Paravahera. *Buddhist Meditation in Theory and Practice*. Kuala Lampur: Buddhist Missionary Society, 1975.

Wilber, Ken. *One Taste: Daily Reflections on Integral Spirituality*. Boston: Shambhala, 2000.

Yogananda, Paramahansa. *Spiritual Diary*. Los Angeles: Self-Realization Fellowship, 1982.

Donald Altman is a former Buddhist monk and award-winning writer. He conducts nationwide "Mindful and Sacred Eating" workshops and retreats based on his book *Art of the Inner Meal*. He also lectures and teaches about mindful living and bringing spiritual values into daily life. Donald trained with the Venerable U Silananda, author of *The Four Foundations of Mindfulness*, at a Buddhist monastery located near the San Bernardino Mountains in Southern California. He has taken monastic vows twice during intensive retreat periods— a practice common in many Southeast Asian countries—and hopes to do so again. He is a member of the Dzogchen Foundation and the Burma Buddhist Monastery Association.

A prolific writer whose career spans more than twenty years, Donald has written for children's television, documentaries, and has had articles featured in publications such as *New Age Journal* and *Magical Blend*. He has published several books, taught writing at Colorado Mountain College, and lectured on writing at California State University, Northridge. Presently, he is completing graduate studies in psychotherapy at Lewis and Clark College, and is working on an inspirational novel called *Monk in My Backyard*. An avid motorcyclist, Donald enjoys riding along the Oregon coast. He lives in Portland, Oregon, with his wife and two cats.

Inner Ocean Publishing

Expanding horizons
with books that
challenge the mind,
inspire the spirit,
and nourish the soul.

We invite you to visit us at:
www.innerocean.com

Inner Ocean Publishing, Inc.
PO Box 1239, Makawao
Maui, HI 96768, USA
Email: info@innerocean.com